101 Hilarious
PRANKS
AND PRACTICAL JOKES

Plus, Learn to Invent Your Own!

WRITTEN BY
THERESA JULIAN,
WHO TRIED THE "DROP YOUR HEAD" PRANK
AND CAN'T FIGURE OUT WHERE IT WENT

ILLUSTRATED BY
PAT LEWIS,
WHO'S <u>STILL</u> CLEANING THE BALONEY
OUT OF HIS SHOES

Odd Dot　　　New York

TO MOM AND DAD, WITH LOVE
AND TO ALL PARENTS WHO ARE BRAVE ENOUGH
TO PICK UP A PRANK BOOK —T.J.

TO MY WIFE, MY PARENTS, AND
SOREN SORENSEN ADAMS (LOOK HIM UP!) —P.L.

Odd Dot

An imprint of Macmillan Publishing Group, LLC
120 Broadway, New York, NY 10271
OddDot.com

Library of Congress Cataloging-in-Publication Data is available.
ISBN: 978-1-250-76844-5

DESIGNER Phil Conigliaro
EDITOR Justin Krasner

Our books may be purchased in bulk for promotional,
educational, or business use. Please contact your local bookseller
or the Macmillan Corporate and Premium Sales Department at
(800) 221-7945 ext. 5442 or by email at
MacmillanSpecialMarkets@macmillan.com.

Printed in the United States of America by
LSC Communications, Crawfordsville, Indiana

First edition, 2021
3 5 7 9 10 8 6 4 2

DISCLAIMER: READING THIS BOOK MAY CAUSE INTENSE LAUGHTER

If you're looking for a long, boring book that will put you to sleep, this is not for you. You also may not like this if you think books should be filled with useful information. This book has nothing of the sort. Instead, it's jam-packed with mindless tricks, kooky nonsense, and lots and lots of silly pranks.

Only read this book if you want to learn completely ridiculous skills, such as how to use goofy faces, funny voices, bad smells, weird sounds, and smooth body moves to trick your friends. We also can't promise that you won't get frosting in your hair when your friend slices into an exploding cake or that the stories about wiggly ear disease and fried brain dust are real. But this is a prank book, so believe only what you see. Or half of what you read. Better yet, don't believe any of it. It's all made up.

TABLE OF
DISCONTENTS

PRANKS, PRACTICAL JOKES, AND USELESS SKILLS YOU CAN'T LIVE WITHOUT

WARNING! The **S**chool of **H**ijinks, **M**alarkey & **O**utlandish **P**ranks (**SHMOP**) is a perilous place! Enter at your own risk!

SHMOP is a top-notch institution that teaches the fine art of pranking and practical joking. Take a tour of our school and you'll become a pro at pretending your finger broke off, filling your friend's doughnut with sour cream, putting bubble wrap under the toilet seat, and more! **SHMOP** will help you pull epic pranks by teaching you about **physical comedy**, which is using your body to make someone laugh. We'll explain how to use funny faces, strange voices, weird smells, and mushy bananas to make your pranks extra-awesome.

But beware! If you prank your friends, they may prank you back! After reading this book, you may never sit down again without first checking to see if fake poop is on your chair. You may never slip your hands into your jacket pockets again without patting them first for plastic spiders. You may never put on your shoes again without glancing to see if they're filled with a pound of baloney.

DO NOT turn the page unless you're ready. *Really ready.*

WAIT!

STOP!

Get your finger off the edge of the . . .

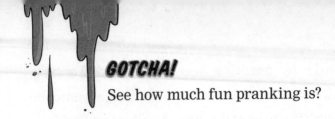

GOTCHA!

See how much fun pranking is?

Since you had the guts to turn the page, you've proved yourself a perfect recruit for **SHMOP**. Keep reading to become a successful prankster. Check out our pranks, try a few, practice them, and pay attention. There's a quiz at the end that'll let you know if you're plucky enough to be a **Prank Master Supreme**.

Now clean the dead fish off your head, wipe the tomato mush off your nose, and read the following pledge. Sorry about the extra step, but ever since that kid slipped into a bucket of buttered noodles, we have to ask this.

THE PRANK RESPONSIBLY PLEDGE

I promise to prank responsibly. I will:

PULL PRANKS THAT ARE FUNNY BUT <u>NOT MEAN.</u>
My pranks will never hurt someone's feelings or make someone look bad. I prank only to make people laugh—and to make sure my friends know I'm an ace at pulling a worm out of my nose.

PRANK SOMEONE WITH A SENSE OF HUMOR.*
If I'm visited by old Aunt Helen, who just had her hip replaced, I will not jump out at her wearing my bloody zombie mask. Instead, I'll use common sense and save that prank for my brother.

NOT RUIN STUFF.
I promise not to ruin things, especially stuff that belongs to teachers who can flunk me, cranky neighbors who can yell at me, and camp counselors who can make me scrub the toilets with an old toothbrush.

CLEAN UP.
I will not be a pea brain and forget to clean up. I may forget how to make ice cubes that *don't* contain fake mouse turds, but I will never forget to clean up.

BE CAREFUL!
I will read the pranking instructions carefully and follow all the warnings. If I break my pledge (or any body part), I will not sue the awesome, talented, prank-loving people who created this book.

* **Never** pull a food-related prank on someone who has a food allergy. Also, only prank someone who is sure-footed and won't be so surprised they'll fall over or get hurt. Be careful not to prank someone who's having a hard time. Keep your eye on the person you're pranking, and make sure they're laughing along. If they're not, stop right away. Apologize, then don't do it again. We joke about a lot of things in this book, but we're not joking about this!

LIVING ON THE RAGGED EDGE:
SWAGGER, STRUT, AND ATTITUDE

DR. CRANKSHAW

AH! A new recruit!

I can tell you're a newbie because you're fresh-faced and smiling—and your hair isn't streaked with ketchup, your shirt isn't coated with fake vomit, and your real fingers are still attached—which, by the way, could be different if you'd like to make some changes.*

I'm Dr. Prankshaw, headmaster of **SHMOP**. I'm a scientist, inventor, and 63-year-old genius, but if wisdom counts, I'm more like

---

* See page 90 to learn how to pretend to bite off your finger.

318. Some people say I resemble Dr. Crankshaw from the Laugh Lab, which is the impressive establishment next door that teaches kids how to create their own jokes.** But just because we're both tall and devilishly handsome—and our names rhyme—doesn't mean I'm his brother. Or his cousin. Or that I'm really Dr. Crankshaw, just with glasses and a funny nose, because that would be *ludicrous*.

Ignore the fact that this giant contraption just called me Dr. Crankshaw. I'm definitely Dr. *Prankshaw*.

YES, DR. CRANKSHAW, THAT WOULD BE LUDICROUS

L.O.L.A.

WHOOZY-WHATZY pat. pending

25¢

** Want to learn how to create your own jokes and become instantly funny? Check out *The Joke Machine*, a book that teaches you how to be funny and make your friends and family LOL. (If you're wondering if you need another book on how to have fun and make people laugh, the answer is yes, you do. You *really* do.)

7

This hodgepodge of steel, plastic, and electronics is my invention, **LOLA**, which stands for **L**augh **O**ut **L**oud **A**pparatus.

She's perturbed because I'm making her work two jobs. At the Laugh Lab next door, **LOLA** creates jokes, and here at **SHMOP**, she creates pranks. No kidding! Just toss a whoopee cushion, rubber snake, and mustard packet into **LOLA** and she'll spit out a funny prank. Want to learn how to make fart noises under your arm? **LOLA** will teach you. Want to convince your parents that you're now a lawyer? **LOLA** will explain. Want to know what all those school supplies in your desk drawer are for? Well, uh, that we can't answer, but if you want to learn how to smash an orange slice through your head, you've come to the right place.

WHOOZY-WHATZY
pat. pending

Are you ready, **LOLA**? Let's teach our new recruit the first thing to know when pranking.

EEK.
UGH. GRRRREEP
ATTITUDE

Ah! She says the most basic thing you need when pranking is to develop an **attitude**. How would you feel in the prank situation? If you're pretending you've just won a million dollars, act flabbergasted. If you're pretending a tooth has fallen out, act shocked. If you've filled the cabinet with ping-pong balls, act casual as you wait for someone to open the door. Pick an attitude, commit to it, and really **sell it**.

Now, let's try **LOLA** again. Give us an example of a prank with lots of 'tude!

MUNCHING ON VOMIT! THAT'S WHERE YOU NEED TO START!

MUNCH ON VOMIT

Yum! A gooey pile of vomit. Vomit's as delicious as grandma's meat loaf—because it *is* grandma's meat loaf—and a bunch of other things. This prank involves pouring a food mixture onto the floor, pretending it's vomit, and eating a few chunks in front of a horrified friend.

Ingredients

- Mixing bowl
- Spoon and fork
- Food. Use whatever food is in your fridge or cabinets to achieve a ghoulish greenish-brown sludge. Foods that work well are peas, green juice, oatmeal, brown cereal, old bananas, and tuna fish.

Action

1. Put the food in the bowl.

2. Mash it with the fork, then stir it with the spoon. Keep the goop at room temperature until you're ready to pull the prank.

3. Clean a small section of the floor where you're going to pour the mush, because you're going to literally *eat off the floor*.

PULL THE PRANK

 When your friend is in one room, pour the fake vomit onto the floor in another room.

> ⚠ Pour the vomit on a floor that you can easily clean, such as tile or linoleum, not a rug or carpet that can stain or get chunks stuck in it.

 With a shocked attitude, scream as if a tarantula just bit your toe.

 When your friend runs into the room, gasp and point at the gross mixture.

 Make up a story, such as the dog or your little brother must have barfed.

 Gradually change your attitude to curiosity in the vomit. Move closer to it, calmly bend down, pick up the biggest chunk, and chew on it thoughtfully. With a straight face, comment on its scrumptious taste. Say that, from its taste, you can tell it came from the dog.

 If your friend hasn't fainted yet, eat another chunk. Lick your fingers, too.

That's a bang-up, or should I say *barf-up*, prank! Did you notice how the prankster started with a shocked attitude, then switched to curiosity? The contrast between the two very different 'tudes makes it funny.

Four Fabulous Suggestions on Attitude

Before you pull a prank, find the attitude. Once you choose the right one, everything flows naturally from it: facial expressions, body language, and tone of voice. To find the perfect attitude:

Brainstorm different attitudes, such as being sad, mad, glad, or *rad*! Don't always go with the first thought that pops into your head. Sometimes the funniest is the *opposite* of what you'd expect, such as pretending nothing's wrong when something bizarro happens.

Adjust accordingly. Think about the whole prank from beginning to end. You can:

- Keep the same attitude throughout the prank.

- Start with one attitude, and move to another, the way the prankster did in the Munching on Vomit trick.

- Escalate the attitude, such as starting off cautiously and growing the fear as the situation gets stickier.

- Tone it down, if you're pranking someone who seems really afraid, angry, or nervous. Remember, pranks are meant to be funny, never mean.

Exaggerate, but keep it believable. If you're pretending you've just cracked your nose, act as if you're in pain. Stretch the emotion so it grabs your friend's attention but not so much that it's preposterous.

Use your whole body. If you're surprised, your eyes fly open, your shoulders roll back, and your hands fly up.

Now dive into these pranks that all use lots of 'tude!

EXPLODING CAKE

Picture this: It's your friend's birthday, and she's sitting in front of her cake, all smiles. After everyone sings "Happy Birthday," she picks up the cutter and pushes it into the cake, waiting to see the luscious strawberry filling you said was in it. But does she ever get to see the filling? Sadly, no, because the thing in front of her is not really a cake; it's an iced balloon resting in a cake pan. So when she cuts into it . . . *POP!*

Ingredients

- A medium-size round balloon
- A round cake pan
- 16-ounce canister of icing
- Blunt knife
- OPTIONAL: Cake decorations, such as sprinkles and candy flowers

Action

1. Use the blunt knife to cover the bottom of the pan with icing.

2. Blow up the balloon so it's almost the size of the pan.

3. Gently push the balloon into the icing in the pan. The icing will act like glue and hold the balloon in place.

4. Use the knife to gently ice the balloon.
   Cover every inch of the balloon that's visible.
   OPTIONAL: add decorations.

PULL THE PRANK

 When it's time to sing "Happy Birthday," place the cake in front of your smiling friend.

 When the song is over, hand her the cake cutter with a calm attitude. Then stand back! *Way back!*

15

SPIDERS IN JACKET POCKETS

Did you ever put on your jacket at the beginning of a new season, stick your hands into your pockets, and get grossed out by all the disgusting stuff that had been in there for months? Well, this prank takes that feeling and supersizes it.

Ingredients

About 6–12 plastic spiders, which you can buy at a discount or party store*

Action

When your friend isn't looking, fill up his jacket pockets with spiders.

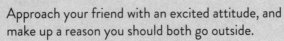

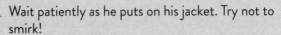 **PULL THE PRANK**

1. Approach your friend with an excited attitude, and make up a reason you should both go outside.

2. Wait patiently as he puts on his jacket. Try not to smirk!

* If you're all out of spiders, use your imagination and try to think of something else that would be equally icky, such as peeled grapes or wet Band-Aids. It doesn't matter what the thing looks like, only what it feels like.

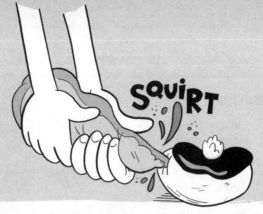

SQUIRT

SOUR CREAM DOUGHNUT

Isn't the cream inside a doughnut luscious? Most people think so, except, of course, if they eat *this* doughnut. Little will your friend know that you squeezed out the doughnut's sweet cream (ate it, of course) and refilled the doughnut with a horrid combination.

Ingredients

- A cream or jelly doughnut that hasn't been eaten (finding one is the hardest park of this prank)

- ¾ cup of sour cream or mayonnaise

- Teaspoon of salt

- Mixing bowl

- Spoon

- Plastic sandwich bag

- Scissors

Action

1. Squeeze out the doughnut's cream, and either eat it or save it for the prank on page 20.

2. Combine the salt and sour cream (or mayo) in the bowl, and mix.

3. Spoon the mixture into the plastic bag.

4. Cut off a corner of the plastic bag, and squeeze the salty sour cream (or mayo) from the bag into the doughnut.

 With a pleasant attitude, offer the doughnut to your friend. Tell her the doughnut was homemade (which it kind of is), using a recipe you found in a book (which is also true). She absolutely has to try it.

 When your friend spits out the doughnut and starts yelling, change your attitude to confusion. You thought the doughnut was still good. Well, at least it was good last spring when Grandma baked it.

Bonus Prank:
COOKIE FILLED WITH TOOTHPASTE

If you haven't had your fill of filling things, scrape the cream out of a chocolate sandwich cookie and squeeze white toothpaste onto the cookie in its place. Then put the cookie back together, and casually offer it to a hungry friend!

 After your friend bites into the cookie, tell him to spit it out, because you shouldn't swallow toothpaste. If he's upset, tell him to look on the bright side—at least his teeth are whiter now.

SWEET CREAMS

Cream is sweet, gooey, and too precious to use in only *one* prank. For this trick, you can use any type of cream, even shaving cream, because it's only going on your friend's face. The best part is, your friend will put the messy stuff on her own face, so she can't blame you. Or will she?

Ingredients

- This is a sleepover prank, so the first thing you need is—you guessed it—a sleeping friend

- A handful of cream

- A feather or something to tickle your friend's face with

1. Once your friend is fast asleep, put the cream in her hand without waking her.

2. Using the feather, tickle her face on the same side that has the hand filled with cream.

3. Eventually, your friend will reach up, touch her face, and, *SPLAT*, spatter herself with cream.

4. Now is when you need attitude. Act offended. Who is she to be sloshing shaving cream all around your nice, clean house? You're a proper family who always keeps the house sparkling.

5. Once she fully wakes up, RUN!

SHOWER IN THE KITCHEN

Most families shower in the bathroom, not the kitchen. But, as you can see, things are different when a prankster's around. For this trick, when someone turns on the water, instead of dripping downward out of the faucet, it will spray right at the person. Voilà! Kitchen shower!

Ingredient

Invisible tape

Action

When no one's looking, wrap the tape around the kitchen sprayer so the button that activates the water is pressed in.

PULL THE PRANK

1. Call someone from your family into the kitchen.

2. Smile at him innocently, and casually ask if he can get you a glass of water. Mention that you'd get it yourself, but you've hurt your hand.

3. Sit back and watch the action! Have a towel (and a smile) ready.

CONTROL GRAVITY

You probably know by now that pranksters are pretty awesome people. But did you know they control gravity? They do, and this trick proves it.

This prank doesn't require any ingredients or prep work, except it's a good idea to read up on gravity so you have fun facts to spout when your friend can't lift her leg!

PULL THE PRANK

 Start by telling your friend that you've learned how to control gravity. Mention a few of the gravity facts you've learned.

 Ask her to lean her left shoulder and leg against a wall.

 Move your hands around her right leg the way a magician would, and mumble a spell. Tap the top of her right foot, and say, "Stay put, you big heavy foot."

 With a confident attitude, announce that she now will not be able to lift her right foot (while also keeping her left side against the wall). Stand back and watch her try!

Bonus Prank:
CONTROL YOUR FRIEND'S FINGER

Don't waste all the cool gravity facts you've learned! Use them again in this prank. Ask your friend to bend his middle finger down and place his hand on a table, with his other fingers touching the table. Now ask him to lift his ring finger. He won't be able to, and you'll be the gravity master once again!

TRY TO LIFT THIS FINGER!

UPSIDE-DOWN GLASS OF WATER

Most people think you can drink only from the top of a glass. We at **SHMOP** are here to say that's nonsense. A true prankster prefers the opening at the *bottom* so when their friend picks up the glass, it's a big, wet, funny surprise!

Ingredients

- Two glasses (one should have a similar width at the top and bottom so when it's upside down, it doesn't look upside down)

- Cardboard or thin cutting board

Action

1. Fill the glass that has the similar top and bottom with water all the way to the top.

2. Put the cardboard or cutting board over the top, flip it quickly, and place it on a countertop.

3. Carefully slide the cardboard or cutting board out so the glass and the water stay on the countertop.

4. Fill the second glass of water, and put it next to the first glass with the opening at the top.

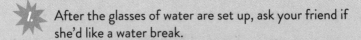

PULL THE PRANK

1. After the glasses of water are set up, ask your friend if she'd like a water break.

2. Walk toward the two glasses. With a nonchalant attitude, pick up the glass that has the opening at the top. Slowly sip your drink.

3. When your friend picks up the other glass and spills it all over herself, ask her to be more careful. It's not polite to dump water all over someone else's kitchen!

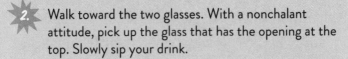

Bonus Prank:
PLASTIC WRAP EXIT

We couldn't *wrap up* this chapter without the "ol' Plastic Wrap Across an Opening" prank. Put a sheet of clear plastic wrap across a door opening, and tape it to both sides of the opening. Then, with a cool and composed attitude, ask your friend to come into the room you're in so he'll have to walk through the door opening you rigged. Then—*eek!* He'll be all wrapped up!

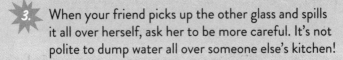

Got that? Good! Developing an attitude is tip-top when starting a prank.

And by the way, it really is me, Dr. Crankshaw from next door! I fooled you, right?! What a prank! Can you believe I kept the story going through the whole chapter? Now head to the next room in **SHMOP**, where there's a lot more nonsense, uh, I mean *learning*.

TELLING A STORY WITH MUSTARD, RELISH, AND A LOT OF BALONEY

AHOY, matey. Captain Blimey here, the sea captain who talks to the fishes. I spent many a starry night with me ears open next to a humpback whale that told boatloads of tall tales and salty stories and even gave lottery tips! The most important thing that motormouthed mammal taught me was that before you prank, create a good story.

I'll never forget the time I told me shipmates a whopper of a tale about how the sky rained magic beans in the sea we was sailing through. Then, in the wee hours, when the ship was still and me mates were asleep, I laid a few pounds of dry beans on the ship's hardtop, which is like the roof, you see. When the ship got a-movin' in the mornin', the beans rolled off the hardtop and rained onto the deck. But it looked as if they were comin' from the sky! Me buddies ran for cover, and I laughed so hard I almost fell off the topside. Do you see how the prank wouldn't have worked if I didn't first reel me mates in with an interestin' story?

Aye! It's important. Now let's see what this fine lass, **LOLA**, has to say about creating a story for your prank.

CAPTAIN BLIMEY, YOU'RE MAKING ME BLUSH! HERE'S A PRANK THAT'S A REAL CLAP OF THUNDER.

A prank about a dead finger! A mighty good hoax on land or sea!

FAVORITE DEAD FINGER

Luckily, you're one of those kids whose family has a creepy dead-finger collection. *And* you're kind enough to let a friend take a look at your favorite one. Too bad she doesn't know it's really your finger squirming around in a box.

Ingredients

- Small cardboard jewelry box
- Scissors
- 6 cotton balls
- Stuff to make your finger look old and gross, such as mud, ketchup, or avocado mush

Action

1. Cut a small hole in the bottom of the box close to one end so your finger fits in the box.

2. Slide your finger into the box, and put the cotton around the sides of your finger.

3. Dot your finger with mud, ketchup, or avocado mush.

4. Put the cover on the box.

PULL THE PRANK

1. Once your finger is in the box with the cover on, approach your friend.

2. Pull her aside, and whisper, "Guess what my family has in our basement?"

3. When she asks what, switch into storytelling mode. Tell her you crept down the creaky basement stairs in your house; opened the rusty door to the back room, which is usually locked; coughed because of the dust; and gagged at the stench of rotting skin. When you turned on the light, you jumped back! There, in a back room in your very own basement, was a dead-finger collection! It was probably your great-grandpa's from the war. You spent hours examining each finger and brought your favorite one to show her.

4. Hold out the box. Slowly take the cover off.

5. As she stares down at your gross finger, move it slightly. Add a quick scream, too.

ARRGHH! That's a mighty fishy tale! See how a prank needs to be wrapped up in a good story? Sail ho to the next page for some tips on how to create and tell a monster of a story.

Create a Good Prank Story

1. **Catchy opening.** Start your story by grabbing your friend's attention with something like: "I'm not supposed to tell you this, but . . ."

2. **Cover the W's.** Make sure to mention: **W**ho is involved, **W**hat's going on, **W**here it's occurring, **W**hen it happened, and **W**hy it's happening.

3. **Exaggerate facts.** Keep things exciting but still believable.

4. **Use details.** The key to creating a believable story is juicy details, such as how a place looked, smelled, and sounded, and how you felt about it.

5. **Keep up the pace.** String facts together so the story moves. Don't get bogged down in too much explanation, rambling, or tangents.

6. **Plan a big reveal**, which is the moment your friend realizes you're pranking. Either stand back and let your friend slowly figure out what's happening or plan a sudden startling action, such as busting your hand through the box to show that it's your (live and still attached) finger in the box.

Tell a Good Prank Story

- **Make eye contact.** Your friends will pay attention more if you look into their eyes as you tell the story. If you're talking to several friends, turn and look at each person.

- **Use your face and body.** Use hand gestures, facial expressions, arm waves, leg wiggles, and other body movements to make the story more interesting.

- **Vary your voice.** Make your voice crack at sad parts. Whisper the scary parts. Talk faster when the story is exciting. If you're pranking that a fish is in your bathtub, pretend it has a German accent. Epic!

- **Speak with confidence.** Sell your story as if it really happened.

- **Lather on emotion.** Keep listeners on the edge of their seats by explaining how your hands shook with fear or how you bounced up and down with joy.

- **Pause.** Stop right before an important or funny point in the story. Pausing emphasizes the next line and makes it funnier or more emotional.

- **Move on.** If your friend doesn't laugh, shrug it off and smile anyway.

Now that you know how to cook up a good story and tell it with a lot of bite, try these pranks!

SNAKES IN THE TOILET

Adults like clean toilets—ones that have no grime, no mildew, and *no snakes*. Too bad for the adults in your house. They don't know yet that some slimy reptiles are slithering around in the family commode. But that's okay, you'll let them know.

Ingredients

A few plastic snakes. If you're all out of snakes, a fake rodent or even black pipe cleaners twisted together will do the trick.

Action

1. Create a whale of a story—one that truly conveys the scary situation in your family commode.

2. Drop the fake snakes or rodent into the toilet.

PULL THE PRANK

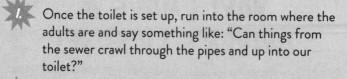

1. Once the toilet is set up, run into the room where the adults are and say something like: "Can things from the sewer crawl through the pipes and up into our toilet?"

2. When an adult asks why you want to know, tell her there are snakes in the toilet. Add details that will make her believe you, such as the number of snakes, their size, and what they look like.

3. As the adult rushes to the bathroom, follow her and keep the story going. For some reason, these snakes are yellow and brown, and you can't understand why they're . . . (Stop there, you *can* understand why.)

4. Once the adult realizes the snakes aren't real, act outraged. What kind of town do you live in? They allow plastic snakes to float through the sewage pipes and up into people's toilets? Tell the adult that that's it, time to move.

YAY! I HAVE A DRIVER'S LICENSE!

Do you know what the DMV is? Of course you don't, you're a kid! DMV stands for Department of Motor Vehicles, and it's the agency that gives you a driver's license. It's also the place where you wait in long lines, get yelled at because you're in the wrong line, get moved to a different line, and then are told to go home because you brought the wrong stuff. But none of that matters. What matters is the DMV made a mistake: They're going to mail you a driver's license even though you're in middle school. *Best mistake ever!*

Ingredient

Letter from the DMV. See page 38.

Action

Photocopy or take a picture of the DMV letter on page 38. Or use some of the wording in the letter and create your own!

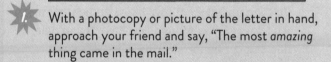

PULL THE PRANK

1. With a photocopy or picture of the letter in hand, approach your friend and say, "The most *amazing* thing came in the mail."

2. After he's finished guessing what it is, tell him about your new driver's license. Say the DMV must have mixed you up with some dude who's actually old enough to drive.

3. Your friend will ask to see the letter. Keep him at bay with excuses such as:

> "I don't want fingerprints on this important paper."

> "I'm going to frame this letter, so it has to stay nice."

> "Get your own driver's license!"

4. When you can't put him off any longer, read the letter and see how long you can keep the story going. If he asks what "DMV" stands for, act surprised. Isn't that something everyone knows?

DEPARTMENT OF MOTOR VEHICLES

Dear New Driver,

We are pleased to inform you that your application for a driver's license has been approved. In a few days you will receive your official license in the mail.

Note that the license is good for up to eight years and that you are required to renew the license upon expiration. Please also note recent changes to motor vehicle laws in our state:

- Pets are no longer allowed to take the steering wheel when you're tired. We have found that dog slobber on the steering wheel creates a slippery, unsafe condition. Cats simply don't have the attention span.

- Eating while driving is no longer permitted. We are aware that fast fast-food fries taste like sheetrock sixty seconds after you get them, but sorry, swallow them *before* getting behind the wheel.

- You are permitted to speak on the phone when driving if you are hands-free. However, you are not allowed to call friends who didn't "like" your post fast enough or failed to comment on your new totally rad skinny jeans, because studies show that those types of conversations result in tense, aggressive driving.

Once again, congratulations on your new license, and please drive carefully!

The Department of Motor Vehicles

YAY! I'M A LAWYER!

Most people have to pay a bazillion dollars and suffer through years of law school to become a lawyer, but not you. Your acceptance letter just dropped in your in-box! For this prank, we at **SHMOP** do hereby declare that you should do what a real lawyer would do: Act prudently, proceed with caution, and save this prank for a more responsible party—your parents.

Ingredient

Letter from Mazey, Mazey, and Yikes.
See page 41.

Action

1. Photocopy or take a picture of the letter on page 41. Or use some of the wording in the letter and create your own!

2. Read the steps on the next page, which explain what to say. Then practice your story so it's believable.

PULL THE PRANK

1. With the letter or photocopy in hand, put on your best flabbergasted face, let out a tiny scream, and run into the room where your parents are.

2. Tell them the law firm of Mazey, Mazey, and Yikes sent you a letter inviting you to join their law firm. When your parents say they don't recognize the name, say the firm is in a fancy building on a busy street in your town.

3. Stare at the letter in confusion. Tell your parents it has your name and address on it, but you're not sure why. If your parents try to take the letter, resist. Say you're still reading it.

4. Tell them the letter asks you to join the law firm as a partner, and it's only going to cost . . . Stop and stare at the numbers. Then say, "Wait, how many zeros is that?" Count the zeros—slowly. Look up and say, "Hmm. A one followed by five zeros. Only $100,000 to join!"

5. Start jumping up and down, and say it would be a blast to be a lawyer. You've seen lots of them on TV, and it looks easy. If they say you have to stay in middle school, remind them that they're talking to a lawyer, someone who could argue the point differently.

6. Once they realize you're pranking, tell them all this debating made you really want to become a lawyer. Tell them to start putting money away because law school is expensive.*

---

*Or tell them you now want to be a doctor. That costs even more.

Dear Prospective Partner,

Mazey, Mazey, and Yikes are pleased to extend an invitation for you to join our law firm as a partner. We invite only 1 percent of attorneys in our area to join, so congratulations on being selected.

We are impressed with your record and all you've accomplished, and the distinguished partners at our firm would be honored to work alongside you.

In case you are wavering between offers, please note that our firm has a snack cabinet filled with cookies and imported treats that we think (but in no way guarantee) you will like. Furthermore, we have an office dog named Jake whose positive traits include (but are not limited to) friendly greetings, demonstrative tail wags, and affectionate snuggles that we find to be (reasonably) helpful after a challenging court case.

Please respond at your earliest convenience with your decision.

Cordially,
THE PARTNERS AT MAZEY,
MAZEY, AND YIKES
A VERRY PROFESSINAL CORPORATION

I. P. MAZEY

SCARY MESSAGE ON THE MIRROR

You've heard the story about the half-man, half-beast who trolls the railroad tracks and breaks into houses, right? You know, the one who's always moaning, "I am Art; I eat hearts." Well, it turns out he's been spotted in your neighborhood today. At least that's the story you can tell your sibling. (Or make up your own creepy tale!) After you tell the story, write the words from the story—such as "I am Art; I eat hearts"—on the bathroom mirror in soap. The message will be invisible when he goes into the bathroom, but after he takes a shower and the room fogs up, Art's words will be clear!

Ingredients

- Bar of soap
- Toilet tissue or napkin

Action

1. Create a good story about Art or your own made-up character. Include details such as why he trolls the tracks, why he eats hearts, and how he became half-man, half-beast.

2. About an hour or two before your sibling takes a shower, write "I am Art; I eat hearts" on the bathroom mirror with a wet bar of soap. At first, the message will be streaky and obvious.

3. Put tissue over your fingers, and trace over each letter. Don't erase the message with the tissue, just smooth it out so it's not visible. But don't worry; once the bathroom is foggy, it will be clear.

 Tell the story about Art to your sibling at least once, with lots of detail. Add creepy voices and frightened faces to really sell the story.

 Before your sibling takes his shower, write the message on the mirror.

 After the shower, stand outside the bathroom and wait for the scream!

A FORTUNE FULL OF WATER

We predict you're going to like this prank because it involves pretending you're a fortune-teller. Tell your friend that his future includes a great deal of water. Maybe a terrible storm is coming? A hurricane? Torrential rain? When he gets worried, suggest that a drink may calm him down. Point to the water bottle you've set up. When he picks up the bottle—which you've pinpricked in a sly way—he'll get soaked . . . as you predicted!

Ingredients

- Water bottle made of thin plastic
- Pin

Action

1. If the water bottle isn't full, fill it to the very top and put the lid back on.

2. Prick the bottle in a downward motion, like this:

3. Make sure the pin goes through the plastic. Do this until you have about twenty-four pricks in a few rows all the way around the bottle. Water will drip out as you do this, but that's okay. Once you set the bottle down, it will stop dripping.

4. Put the water bottle on the desk or table where you'll prank your friend. Wipe off the water that's seeped out so no water is visible on the outside of the bottle.

PULL THE PRANK

 1. With the water bottle on the desk, ask your friend to have a seat. Tell him you'd like to read his fortune.

 2. Close your eyes and tap your head, as if you're thinking. Then tell him you see a great flood entering his life. The flood might be a hurricane or a tsunami, but either way, you're getting a vibe that it will involve a lot of water.

 3. When he looks worried, point to the water bottle. Maybe a drink may make him feel better?

4. When he wraps his hand around the bottle and squeezes it, he'll get sprayed with the water you predicted!

Bonus Prank:
SODA DRIBBLE

Water bottles aren't the only thing you can punch holes in! Use a pin to punch holes in the aluminum soda can your friend is drinking from when she's not looking. Punch them right below the opening. Then, when she brings the can to her face, soda will dribble out of the holes and onto her shirt!

RIP UP A TEST

Teachers make a big deal about important tests. Before you take a test, they're always saying "You need to study" and "Don't forget the test is tomorrow." Then after you take it, they say, "Get the test signed" and "Don't lose it." They never say, "Can you please rip it up?" Of course not. But that's okay, because we'll say it for them. We don't mean really rip up a test, we mean pretend to, just to make your teacher laugh!

Ingredients

- A teacher who likes to laugh and has a good sense of humor (don't pull this on a teacher who hasn't had his morning coffee yet!)

- A test or important homework assignment

Action

1. Practice these steps a few times, because you don't really want to rip up a test!

2. Hold the paper up to your face.

3. At the same time:

- Blow down onto the top of the paper.

- Pull your fingers downward to make a "ripping" sound.

PULL THE PRANK

 Approach a teacher you have a good relationship with. Tell him how much you like his class. Add that you loved studying for the last test because the subject matter was just so interesting. In fact, you're bummed the test is over.

 Take out your test, look up at your teacher with a sad face and say, "That's it. I want to take the test again!"

 Turn your back, and add, "Don't look. This will be painful to watch!" Then make the wicked ripping sound.

 Turn back around, while keeping the test behind your back.

Once your teacher realizes that you're pranking him, ask if there's extra credit for such a great trick. Who knows, maybe he'll say yes!

NOT EVERYONE WILL GET YOUR PRANK

Some people may think your prank is amazing, and others may think it's lame. No matter the reaction, don't take it personally and don't get bummed. Everyone likes different things and laughs at different things. Move on, and try other pranks on other people.

FRIED BRAIN
DUST DISORDER

Fried brain dust disorder (FBDD) is a serious illness that afflicts many pranksters. Studies show that concentrating on pranks for long periods of time causes the brain to slowly disintegrate into a fine powder. This powder, commonly known as fried brain dust, eventually leaks from holes in a prankster's head (mostly through the nose and ears) and causes huge messes on pranksters' floors. Though FBDD is fascinating, we'd like you to know it's also completely made up. We made it up so you'd keep reading and try this prank, which involves coughing powder at your friend and telling her it's fried brain dust.

Ingredient

A fistful of baby powder, flour, or baking powder

Action

Make up a good story about fried brain dust, which is something you can say you've been reading about in those fancy scientific journals.

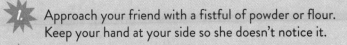

PULL THE PRANK

1. Approach your friend with a fistful of powder or flour. Keep your hand at your side so she doesn't notice it.

2. Start telling her about fried brain dust, the tiny white particles that flake off the brain when it overheats from overuse. Scientists think this happens often. They say you can sometimes see the white particles falling out of someone's nose, mouth, or ears.

3. Mention that, come to think of it, your head's been hurting and that you have been studying a lot. Twitch a little, as if your brain were really disintegrating.

4. When your friend asks what's wrong, hold up your hand so she can't see the powder and cough into it so the powder flies at her.

   ⚠️ Make sure you cough outward! Do not breathe the powder in.

5. Regain your composure, and apologize for covering her with fried brain dust. It's clear your brain is frying from overuse. You wish it weren't, because you can use all the brain cells you can get. Lucky for her, she now has a few more. Too bad they're on her shirt.

49

I'M JUST BACK FROM AN ALIEN ABDUCTION

Did you know aliens are afraid of the dark? And they don't have necks? And they smell like soup? Wow, you know very little about aliens. Time to sharpen your alien awareness so you can pull off this out-of-the-world prank, which is convincing your friend that you've just returned from an alien abduction.

Ingredients

- An empty water bottle that isn't see-through
- Green juice

Action

1. Fill the water bottle with green juice.

2. Use your imagination, and make up a story about the abduction. Try to figure out:

- Where the abduction occurred, such as in a cornfield. If you don't live near a cornfield, say it occurred in an empty parking lot or deserted location. (Aliens don't walk down Main Street.)

- Come up with a good description of what the aliens looked like. Was their skin the usual green we associate with aliens or was it blue or even purple?

- How did they talk? Was it in a mumbled language or was it just sounds?

- What were you thinking during the abduction? Were you wondering: Why do they want me? How bad is it on their planet?

- Did you escape or did they let you go? Maybe they kept trying to read your mind, but you were really lucky because the scan kept coming up blank.

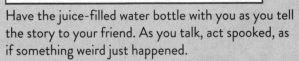

PULL THE PRANK

1. Have the juice-filled water bottle with you as you tell the story to your friend. As you talk, act spooked, as if something weird just happened.

2. Every once in a while, look over your shoulder in fear. Then stop and listen, as if you've just heard something.

3. When your friend starts doubting your story, reach for the water bottle.

4. Take a sip, but don't swallow the juice. Instead, bend over as if you're in pain. Let the juice dribble out of your mouth. Shout about how it's starting to happen. The aliens are taking over your body!

Got all of that, matey? Now get out there and walk the planks. I mean *rock your pranks*!

PREPPING, PROWLING, AND WAITING FOR THE PEE TO STOP

HELLO, friend! Just because you can't see me doesn't mean you should be afraid. I'm here to tell you how important it is to pace yourself, step carefully, and wait for just the right minute to . . .

BOO!

. . . *Surprise* your friend that he's being pranked! Good pranks need prepping, practice, prowling, pacing, and patience, which means they require a lot of *p*'s, and sometimes even pee, but what I'm here to talk about is pacing and patience. A good prank starts off slowly and builds to an emotional *KABOOM*.

Picture this: Your mother walks into the kitchen and hasn't yet seen the fake tarantula on the cheese casserole. Do you jump up and yell, "Mom, look at the cheese casserole, ha ha!"? No, of course not. You sit and wait, distract her with comments about how good you've been (which, you know, is *always true*), and wait for the time to be ripe. It's sooo much better if she finds the hairy spider herself!

And don't let your face or body language hint that you're about to reveal the prank.

Okay, we've waited long enough! It's time for **LOLA** to astonish us with a prank that needs pacing and patience!

What are you waiting for, **LOLA**? Give us a prank.

I'M JUST TAKING YOUR ADVICE, WAITING FOR THE TIME TO BE RIGHT.

C'mon, **LOLA**, we need a prank! We're running out of page!

FINE, YOU WANT A PRANK WITH A LOT OF P'S? HERE YOU GO!

NEVER-ENDING PEE

Stopping to pee is a pain when you're playing video games or doing homework. Luckily, peeing usually takes less than a minute. We say *usually* because, with this prank, it takes a lot longer. *A lot longer.* For this prank, you'll go into the bathroom and pour long drizzles of water into the toilet so it sounds as if

you're peeing for three minutes. Or four. Or, if you really want to shock her socks off, twenty!

Pre-Prank Prep

Ingredients

Three large glasses of water

Action

Before your friend comes over, hide the glasses of water somewhere in the bathroom.

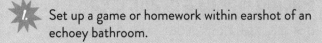

1. Set up a game or homework within earshot of an echoey bathroom.

2. Once your friend is comfortable and not suspecting anything, tell her you have to go to the bathroom.

3. After you've closed the bathroom door, slowly drizzle a glass of water into the toilet. Then pause, and say something like: "Wow, I shouldn't have had five cans of soda."

4. Pour another glass of water into the toilet. After ten seconds, stop and say, "And I shouldn't have had a half gallon of chocolate milk."

5. Pour more water into the toilet. Continue pouring, talking, and pausing to keep the prank going at a good pace. After you've emptied all three glasses, you can refill them from the sink and truly make this prank go on forever.

6. When you think your friend is running out of patience, stop and say, "Have you ever seen a toilet overflow?"

When the pee prank *finally* ends, turn the page to learn more about pacing out a prank!

YOUR TURN!

Six Smashtabulous Timing and Rhythm Tips

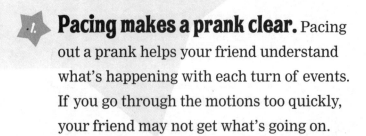

1. **Pacing makes a prank clear.** Pacing out a prank helps your friend understand what's happening with each turn of events. If you go through the motions too quickly, your friend may not get what's going on.

2. **Well-paced pranks are funnier.** If you're pranking that you're killing an imaginary spider, swat it, then look under your shoe to make sure you got it. Hop around. Swat it again. Pretend it's still alive, run across the room. Swat it again, etc.

3. **Keep cool throughout.** It's hard not to flinch when you know a pie to the face is coming, but it's much funnier when it looks as if you're completely surprised.

4. Pause before the big reveal.

Pausing for a second or two creates suspense and makes your friend want to know even more about what's coming.

5. Pause after the big reveal. After you

spring the surprise, be silent for a second so what just happened sinks in.

6. Know when to end. If your friend is

really afraid, or a parent is really mad, that's your cue!

HEAD LICE ARE DELICIOUS

Head lice are tiny white insects that nest in your hair, suck your blood, itch your skin, lay eggs on your scalp—and surprisingly, are delicious. That is, delicious when you *pretend* to eat them, not really eat them, because that would be just plain gross—which makes this an excellent prank. Yum!

Ingredient

A small piece of white food, such as a Tic Tac, a coconut flake, or a white cookie crumb

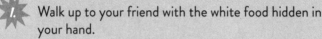

1. Walk up to your friend with the white food hidden in your hand.

2. Listen as your friend tells one of his long, boring stories. (The hardest part of this prank is waiting and keeping up the guise that you're interested in your friend's long story about not finding his math book. At least that's what we think his story was about. We don't know; we weren't listening.)

3. Every few minutes, scratch your head. Scratch casually at first, then start scratching harder and more frequently.

4. Eventually, feel your head with the hand that's holding the white food. Pretend to rip it out of your hair.

5. Glance into your hand, and say, "Holy hello! I have head lice!" Then pop it into your mouth.

6. Chew slowly, in an exaggerated way, as if you were moving a thick piece of steak around in your mouth.

7. Comment on the little bugger's delectable flavor. You've heard that they taste like licorice, but apparently, they taste more like candied pork belly.

LIVE HAND IN THE POPCORN

We at **SHMOP** love the buttery taste of popcorn. It's salty and crunchy and usually doesn't reach out and grab us. But you should know by now that things are different when pranksters are around. This trick involves cutting a hole in the bottom of a bucket of popcorn and sticking your hand up through the middle. Then offer your unsuspecting friend some popcorn. He'll munch away until . . . a hand reaches out from the popcorn and grabs him!

Ingredients

- A bucket or large paper cup filled with popcorn
- A sharp pen to poke a hole in the bottom of the bucket or cup

Action

1. If you're at the movies, tell your friend to go into the theater and get seats while you buy popcorn.

2. Once you have the popcorn, walk toward a trash can because this could get messy!

3. Eat a few handfuls off the top, then take out the pen and poke a hole in the bottom of the tub.

4. Tear the hole wider until it's big enough to stick your hand through. Push your hand into the bucket quickly so the least amount of popcorn spills out.

PULL THE PRANK

 Once your hand is in the popcorn bucket, go into the theater and find your friend.

 Offer him some of your snack. Here's where you need patience and pacing. You may be tempted to reach up right away and grab his hand, but don't! Let him have a few peaceful handfuls first.

 Once he feels your hand, reach up and grab him!

61

KETCHUP MUSTARD SODA

Here's another food-related prank, because we at **SHMOP** believe that playing with food never gets old. This prank involves inserting the bottom of your friend's soda straw into a ketchup or mustard packet so she slurps up a salty condiment instead of the sweet drink she's expecting. Try a relish packet, too. You'll *relish* the results.

Pre-Prank Prep

Ingredient

A ketchup, mustard, or relish packet

Action

1. When you're with a friend who's drinking from a straw, sit back and act natural.

2. When she gets up to go to the bathroom or check something, rip the end of a condiment packet and insert her straw into the packet.

3. Put the packet and straw back into her drink, and make it look as if the drink wasn't touched.

PULL THE PRANK

 When your friend comes back to the table, act as if nothing happened. Don't mention her drink, just wait for her to take another sip. If time goes by and she hasn't reached for her drink, sip yours and comment on how good it is. (If your friend observes you enjoying your drink, she'll want to sip her drink, too.)

 When she finally takes a drink and spits out the condiment, tell her that she needs to mind her manners. Fine-dining establishments do not allow yelling and spitting.

⚠️ Touch your friend's straw only if you have clean, just-washed hands. Spreading germs is not a joke!

Bonus Prank:
HOW KNOT TO DRINK

If your friend has forgotten the previous prank and is brave enough to drink through a straw in your presence, here's another prank to try. If she leaves for a minute, take the straw out, tie a knot in the bottom of it, and put it back in the drink. When she returns, wait for her to try the drink now!

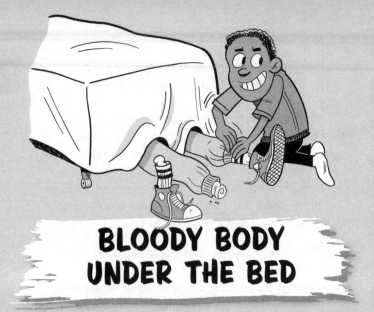

BLOODY BODY UNDER THE BED

Lots of kids have gross stuff under their beds: dust bunnies, dirty socks, retainers, cookie crumbs, and . . . a dead body? Well, not the whole body, just the bloody legs. Well, not *real* legs, fake ones, made of pants stuffed with towels and dotted with ketchup blood—a sight that's guaranteed to scare *the pants* off your friend.

Ingredients

- Pants
- A pair of socks
- A pair of shoes
- Things to stuff the pants with, such as towels, paper, or clothes
- OPTIONAL: Ketchup

Action

1. Stuff the legs of a pair of pants with towels or clothes. Slide the pants under the bed so only the bottom half shows.

2. Stuff a pair of socks with similar items, and put the stuffed socks into a pair of shoes.

3. Slide the socks (with the shoes attached) into the leg openings at the bottom of the pants.

4. Sprinkle ketchup on the fake legs for a bloody look.

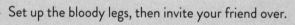

1. Set up the bloody legs, then invite your friend over.

2. After time has passed, ask if he heard a sound in the bedroom where the legs are. He'll probably say no and get back to what you were doing.

3. About ten minutes later, ask again. When he says no, go back to what you were doing.

4. About ten minutes later, stop and say this time you're sure you heard something. Since you're a mature and responsible kid, you need to stop and check it out, you know, for the safety of your entire family.

5. Point your friend toward the bedroom with the bloody legs, and let him go first.

6. When he screams and runs out of the room, either:

   - Scream, too, and spout questions, such as "Who died under my bed?"

   - Act as if it's no big deal. More bloody legs? Must be Tuesday.

Bonus Prank:
SCARY SURPRISE

This chapter wouldn't be complete without the ol' "hiding patiently under the bedcovers and jumping out at the person who tries to wake you" trick. But don't just hide under the covers any old way, hide with your Halloween mask on, an eye patch over your eye, or some other surprising costume. That'll scare the willies out of them!

What Is Physical Comedy?

Physical comedy is using your body to make someone laugh. An example is hopping on one foot like a crooked pogo stick when you're pretending you've stubbed your toe. Sometimes you can get a laugh with no words—just physical craziness—and sometimes silly body movements add to your words and make them funnier.

CALL YOUR FRIEND ON A SMELLY SHOE

Why pay for an expensive cell phone when you've got a smelly shoe? Pretend to call your friend on a shoe while someone, like your sister, can hear. Talk into your shoe in a made-up language. When the friend you were pretending to talk to stops by and references what you were just saying to your shoe, your sister will want a cool shoe phone, too!

Ingredient

A smelly shoe

Action

1. Ask a friend to pull the prank and learn Op language with you. To speak Op:

   Spell every word out loud, adding the "op" sound after every consonant. Don't add anything after vowels. For example, *hello* in Op is:

   "Hop e lop lop o"

In Op, the sentence *I like pranking* is:

"I lop i kop e pop rop a nop kop i nop gop."

2. Figure out a time when your friend will ring the doorbell and what you'll pretend the conversation will be about.

PULL THE PRANK

1. Start the prank a few minutes before your friend will knock on the door.

2. When your sister, or the person you want to prank, is near, start speaking into your shoe in Op.* Throw in a few sentences in English too so she gets the gist of what you're talking about.

3. Pretend to press a button on your shoe, as if you were hanging up. When your sister asks what you were doing, tell her you were talking to your friend, of course, and mention the topic of the conversation. If she seems surprised, tell her you downloaded an app that turns a shoe into a cell phone. Hasn't she heard of it?

4. When your friend rings the doorbell, let him in and act as if nothing is wrong. Discuss the best movie of all time, or whatever topic you've agreed to, and throw in some words in Op, too. Watch your sister scratch her head!

* If your shoe is *too* smelly, call your friend on a banana, a can of hair spray, or a tube of toothpaste.

INSECT-INFESTED TOILET PAPER

The one place people can count on to always be peaceful is the bathroom. No one bothers you when you're in there. Even if someone knocks on the door, a simple "I'm in here" makes them go away. Well, peace in your bathroom is about to change. When the next person in your family reaches for the toilet tissue, he'll unroll insect-infected paper!

Ingredient

A black marker, not a pen (a pen will rip the toilet paper)

Action

1. Unroll a few feet of toilet tissue, and lay it flat on the bathroom floor.

2. Skip the first seven squares. Then start drawing insects on the eighth, ninth, tenth, and eleventh squares. You can draw the insects freehand or trace the insects below:

3. Roll the paper back up. The first few squares, which are still all white, should be the outer sheets so you can't see the insects.

4. If you can see the insects through the top layer, tear off a clean white section of toilet paper from a different roll and lay it over the first roll. We really want your family to be surprised!

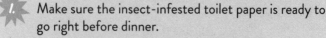

1. Make sure the insect-infested toilet paper is ready to go right before dinner.

2. During dinner, casually mention that you saw some big black bugs in the bathroom. There's no need for anyone to worry, you were brave and killed them all.

3. Then, throughout dinner, spout random insect facts. Did you know there are spiders in 68 percent of the world's bathrooms? An ant can carry fifty times its body weight. A fly's favorite things to eat are cow dung, mice brains, and Twinkies—in that order. None of these facts are important, and some aren't even true, but that's okay. What's important is that you keep your family thinking about gross insects as they eat.

4. When dinner's over, keep an eye on the bathroom and wait for the fireworks!

If you're still in the mood to draw insects, trace the insect shapes on paper; color them black, brown, or gray; and cut them out. Gently tape the bugs to the inside of a lampshade. When someone turns on the light, it will look as if creepy bugs are crawling all over the lampshade!

Now that you're an expert at pacing, slip into the next room to learn how to use goofy faces in your pranks!

KOOKY EXPRESSIONS, CRAZY EYES, AND OTHER WAYS TO TALK WITH YOUR FACE

WHO needs words when you've got a face? Hi, I'm Ace the Face, and you guessed it, I'm all about faces. I love ones that are surprised, sad, mad, glad, *rad*—and everything in between. Let's face it, expressions are key to a successful prank because they really help *sell* your story. Picture a face with a nervous tic or one with hulking eyes and a crooked mouth that says *gee gads!* The look on your face can grab someone's attention; it can say a lot more than words and can get a laugh without your uttering a sound. So when you're pranking, let your face do the talking!

Figuring out how to change your expression to show what you're thinking is easy because it comes from *attitude*. Once you commit to an attitude, such as sadness, and really think about being sad, the corners of your mouth droop, your eyes get watery, and your eyebrows knit together. Just relax, and let your attitude shine through!

Now, let's get face-to-face with **LOLA**. What do you have for us?

I ONLY GIVE PRANKS TO PEOPLE I KNOW, AND YOUR FACE DOESN'T RING A BELL.

Ha! **LOLA**'s always teasing me! Okay, **LOLA**, here's the bell: *RINGGG, RINGGG, BBBRINGGG.*

NOW I REMEMBER YOU, OF COURSE! I NEVER FORGET A FACE! HERE'S YOUR PRANK.

A prank where you pretend your eye is leaking! Face-tabulous!

HELP, MY EYE IS LEAKING!

We at **SHMOP** have no idea what eyeballs are made of. They're probably made of tissue, fluid, cells, membranes—and that white elastic that keeps your pants up. The dark part of an eyeball is called the *pupil*, because inside it are tiny students (the smart kind) who tell your brain what you're looking at. That's what we think, but we don't really know. What we do know is that it's funny to pretend your eyeball is leaking.

Ingredient

One of those little white plastic containers that hold coffee creamer

Action

Practice so you can crush the creamer without hurting your eye. To do so:

- Loosen the paper on the top of the creamer so the cream can leak out easily.

- Put the creamer in your hand, and make a gentle fist around it.

- Bring your fist to your eye. Practice rubbing your eye with the back of your hand so no cream gets in your eye.

1. With a creamer hidden in your hand, talk to your friend as if nothing's wrong.

2. Start twitching the eye that's on the same side of your body as the hand that's holding the cream. Gradually increase your twitchiness until your eye seems to be fluttering uncontrollably. Make a worried face.

3. Tell your friend you've been having a lot of trouble with your eye. It's been itchy and painful and always feels hot.

4. Mumble something about how you can't take it anymore, then rub your fist against your eye and slowly crush the creamer. Moan as you do so your friend can't hear the container crushing.

5. As the cream drips down your hand and cheek, crinkle up your face as if you're in pain. When your friend seems concerned, tell him it's okay, you'll just use your other eye from now on. How great is it that you have two?!

Let's *face* facts, that was a great prank!

YOUR TURN!

Practice talking with your face! Sit in front of a mirror, and without words, try making each attitude below show on your face.

AFRAID

You're pretending there's a copper-head snake in the coat closet.

AMAZED

You're trying to convince your friend that instead of the usual $10, Granny put $1,000,000 in your birthday card.

ANNOYED

Your friend changed the spellchecker on your phone, and now you can't even type "Hey there" without it changing to "don't stare."

BORED

You set up a balloon to pop when your friend opens the door, but he's two hours late.

CONFUSED

You're pretending you don't know why the gerbil food is missing. You're trying to prank your parent that the cat ate it.

DISGUSTED

You thought your friend handed you a glass of orange juice, but you tasted it and it's really cheese powder and water.

EMBARRASSED

Your friend put a whoopee cushion on your seat, and you sat on it.

ENERGETIC

You ate a bowl of cereal your brother made, not knowing he put two energy drinks in it.

EXCITED

Your new bag of stick-on scars just came in the mail, and you can't wait to use them.

MAD

 Your brother set up fifteen alarm clocks that all started ringing in your room at six A.M.

SAD

You're pranking your friend that your pet rock died.

INTERESTED

You're reading a book about pranking, and it's the most fascinating book of all time.

PROUD

You've successfully put all your friend's pencils inside a bowl of gelatin.

PEACEFUL

You've received "The World's Best Prankster" award. You hang it on your wall and can't help but smile at it.

PUSH A PENCIL THROUGH YOUR HEAD

This prank makes it look as if you're pushing a pencil up your nose and pulling it out your ear. It's perfect for when a friend asks to borrow a pencil. Not only can you lend him a pencil, but you can also coat it with your superior brain cells and then hand it to him. Boo-yah!

Ingredient

A pencil

Action

Practice this trick in the mirror until you can do it quickly and smoothly:

1. Hold the top of a pencil with one hand (let's say your right hand).

2. Cup your left hand around the bottom of the pencil, and slide your hand upward so it covers the pencil.

3. Bring both of your hands toward your ear. Make sure your left hand still covers the pencil.

4. While your right hand is still holding the top of the pencil, slide your left hand out quickly, so it looks as if you're pulling the pencil out of your ear.

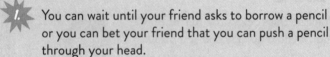

PULL THE PRANK

1. You can wait until your friend asks to borrow a pencil or you can bet your friend that you can push a pencil through your head.

2. Follow the steps above, and make a hideous face as you're doing this trick. Make your face look as it would if you had really pushed a pencil up your nose and out your ear! Grimace, snarl, and sneer.

3. Once you're finished, smile and hand the pencil to your friend. Be sure to mention that it's now covered with extra brain cells. This pencil is sure to score an A on any test.

PUSH YOUR FINGER THROUGH YOUR HEAD

If you think we're finished pushing things through our head, you're wrong. Try the classic "Push Your Finger Through Your Head" trick. For this one, stick your right index finger in your right ear. At the same time, push your tongue against your left cheek. If you do both at the same time, it looks as if your finger is going through your head and pushing out against your cheek!

DEAD FLIES IN THE ICE CUBES

Ice cubes are supposed to be clear, with nothing in them except for ice, right? Well, last month a shelf broke in the **SHMOP** freezer, and the ice cubes fell into the frozen peas. Then all the drinks had little green pea flecks floating in them. We tell you this story as an example of how disgusting it is to have weird things in your ice cubes. To achieve something even *grosser*, we created a prank where you make ice cubes stuffed with raisin bits—which look like dead flies—and drop the cubes in your drink and your friend's. Maybe you can get her *buzzing*?!

Ingredients
- Ice cube tray
- Twelve raisins
- Two see-through glasses

Action

1. Fill the empty ice cube tray halfway to the top with water, then put it in the freezer for two hours.

2. Cut the raisins in half, and squeeze them so the raisin bits are funny shapes and no longer look like raisins.

3. Take the tray out and drop a raisin bit or two in the center of each cube. Fill the tray to the top with water. Put the tray back in the freezer for another two hours.

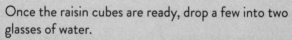

1. Once the raisin cubes are ready, drop a few into two glasses of water.

2. Hand your friend the water with a straight face, and start sipping yours.

3. Don't say anything; just sip your drink with interest. Let your eyebrows fly up, and make a face as if this were the best water you've ever had. Widen your eyes, and look closer at the glass. Nod in approval. Take another sip, then lick your lips.

4. When your friend notices the "flies" and screams, take the glass from her and examine it thoughtfully. Tap your head, and nod as if you just discovered something. Then say, "Who knew bugs tasted so great" or "Time isn't the only thing flying around here."

I DROPPED MY HEAD

Chickens are lucky. After their heads are cut off, they can still run around. Too bad humans can't do that, because it's a pretty cool trick. Or wait . . . can we? If you're a prankster, you can! To pull this off, hide behind a couch and peek up so just your head is showing. Ask a friend to sit next to you with his head tucked down so it can't be seen. When you sit near each other, it will look as if your head is detached and sitting next to your body. Once you and your friend are set up, make a crazy face, as if your head really just rolled off your body, and call someone from your family into the room!

Action

If you have a big mirror or a camera with a timer, practice this so you can see what you both look like. Adjust your bodies to make it look convincing.

1. Duck behind a couch so only your head is showing above the top of the couch.

2. Ask your friend to sit on the top of the couch facing the opposite direction as you.

3. Tell your friend to keep his shoulders back and duck his head down so when a person walks into the room, they can't see his head.

4. Ask your friend to reach over and grab your hair so it looks as if "the body" is trying to grab "the head" and put it back on.

5. Practice making a really way-out face!

PULL THE PRANK

1. You and your friend should take your positions on the couch, as explained above.

2. Start moaning, and call to someone in your family to come quick.

3. When you hear your family member approaching, make a horrid, kooky face—as if your head were really detached from your body. Then hang on to the couch, because there's going to be a scream!

BACK AWAY, I HAVE THE HEEBIE-JEEBIES!

The heebie-jeebies is a rare and dangerous disease that afflicts more pranksters than any other group on earth. It causes strange little red bumps to break out on your skin. The geniuses at **SHMOP** have spent years studying the illness. Miraculously, they found a cure, which turns out is simply soap and water. They discovered the remedy once they realized the heebie-jeebies is only light lipstick on your skin, along with little bumps of glue. Thank you, **SHMOP** geniuses!

Pre-Prank Prep

Ingredients

- Red lipstick or eye shadow
- School glue
- OPTIONAL: Yellow lipstick or eye shadow

Action

Create heebie-jeebie bumps on your face and body. For each little heebie-jeebie:

1. Smear a tiny, light coating of lipstick or eye shadow on your skin.

2. Put a small dot of glue in the middle of the smear.

3. Once the glue dries, dot the top of the bump lightly with yellow or red lipstick or eye shadow.

 Once you're all heebie-jeebied up, approach your friend nervously. Your friend will probably scream and ask what happened.

 Make one side of your face twitch, as if it were really itchy. Put your hand on his shoulder and tell him that, unfortunately, it's contagious. Scrunch up your nose, and make your eyes shutter.

 If he hasn't run away yet, scratch the bumps and act shocked when they come off. Relax, and say, "Wow, looks like this will go away easily after all!"

PULL A WORM OUT OF YOUR NOSE

When you're pulling a worm out of your nose, words aren't necessary. What this situation calls for is yanking, itching, twitching—and lots of funny faces. Those movements and the sight of a worm squirming out of your face are *more than enough* to freak out your friend.

Pre-Prank Prep

Ingredient

Gummy worm (try to find one that's a realistic color, but any color is funny)

Action

Practice this in a mirror:

1. Put the worm in your right palm, and close your hand.

2. Bring your closed hand (and the worm) to your face.

3. Bring your left hand to your face, and slide it slightly under your right hand.

4. With your left hand, latch on to the worm's free end and push it slightly into one nostril. Make a surprised face, as if you really feel a live worm in your nose.

5. Quickly bring your left hand away from your face, pulling the worm outward. At the same time, move your right hand away from your face. Make an astonished face.

 Approach your friend with the gummy worm hidden in your right hand.

 Sniffle, crinkle your nose, and mention that your nose feels itchy.

 Bring your right hand (and the worm) to your face so your friend can't see it. As described, latch on to it with your left hand and pull it away from your face. Make googly faces as you pull.

 After yanking the worm all the way out, smile and say something like: "Wow, it's great that was a worm and not a giant booger!"

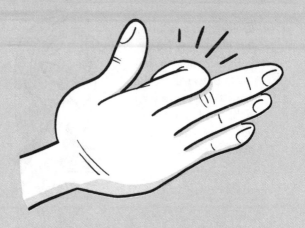

BITE OFF YOUR FINGER

You know that five minutes right before lunch starts, when you're so hungry you could bite off your finger? Well, don't let that time go to waste! Tell your friend you're so famished you can't stand it another minute. Then bite off your finger and have a good chew. Get your whole face into it, as if you were really gnawing on a bone. Swallow, burp, smile, and comment on how surprisingly delicious bone, blood, and skin are.

Action

Practice biting off your finger:

1. Stick the top half of your index finger into your mouth.

2. Gnaw on your finger, and pretend to chomp off the top half.

3. Pull your finger out of your mouth, and study it as if you can't figure out why it won't detach from your hand.

4. Put your finger back into your mouth, and pretend to try harder. Grimace, and let out a tiny yelp, as if you really just bit off half your finger. With an exaggerated gulp, pretend to swallow it.

5. Pull your finger out of your mouth, and hold up your hand with the top half of your index finger bent down.

PULL THE PRANK

 Right before lunch starts, or anytime you and your friends are hungry, start complaining about how famished you are.

 Tell your friends you can't wait another minute. Stick your index finger into your mouth, and start munching. Use facial expressions to sell the trick.

 After "biting" off your finger, proudly show your hand, which now has 4.5 fingers. Announce that you still have 9.5 fingers, which is 95 percent. Not bad. Better than most kids do on the average test.

SMASH AN ORANGE THROUGH YOUR HEAD

Some people think pranksters don't use their heads. That's ridiculous! For this prank, you're not only going to use your head, you're going to pass an orange slice through it. This prank involves betting your friend that you can smash an orange slice against your forehead, move it down through your head, and spit it out of your mouth. Now that's using your head for more than just an earring rack!

Ingredients

Two orange slices (and a hard head)

Action

Practice with the orange slice:

1. Hide one orange slice in your mouth between your teeth and cheek.

 Be careful not to swallow the orange slice!

2. Put the other slice in the palm of your right hand.

3. Secretly switch the slice from your right hand to your left.

4. Take your right hand, which no longer has the orange slice, and smash it against your forehead.

5. Make funny faces, as if the orange slice were really moving down through your head. Then spit out the orange slice that's in your mouth. Ta-da!

PULL THE PRANK

 Hide one orange slice in your mouth, and put the other in your right hand.

 Saunter up to your friend, and announce that you can smash an orange slice through your head.

 Show your friend the slice in the palm of your hand, then distract her. Tell her you don't want to brag about your head's mysterious abilities, but, well, yes you do because your head is really that awesome.

 As you're talking, switch the orange slice to the other hand. Take the hand that doesn't have the orange slice and smash it against your forehead.

 Roll your eyes around as if you're really pushing something through your head. Tilt your head, and make goofy faces.

 Spit out the orange slice in your mouth, and show it to your friend.

Those pranks are **face**-cinating! Turn the page to learn how to get your whole body into a prank.

ARMS THAT WIGGLE AND LEGS THAT JIGGLE

HEY there! Dexter the Toe Texter here, all twisted up to tell you about my special skill—**body language**. Some people communicate with only their voice. Not me! I text with my toes and write with my knees. I even eat with my elbows.

Communicating with your body is a superpower when you're pranking. If you tell your friend the rat in the garage is THIS BIG, **fling** out your arms and show just how big. If you're pretending you're about to vomit, **clutch** your stomach, and double over in pain.

In the prankiverse, body language helps tell a story and paint a picture, and it's usually funnier than words. Like facial expressions, body movements come from *attitude*. A really specific attitude seeps from your brain, into your face, and down through your whole body. If I'm pretending I broke a bone while dialing a phone with my ankle, the pain shows on my entire body: I cradle my ankle, slump my shoulders, and bend over in pain.

Now let's see if **LOLA** can twist up a prank that helps us communicate with our body!

SURE, HERE'S A BODY-BUSTIN' PRANK. JUST STOP TEXTING ME WORDS LIKE SWIMS THAT ARE THE SAME UPSIDE-DOWN. THEY'RE MAKING MY WIRES LOOPY!

LOLA's so funny! She's obviously kidding, because everyone loves words that are the same upside-down. And, look! She gave us a great prank about cracking your neck. **LOLA**, you're the best!

CRACK YOUR NECK

Your neck is an important part of your body. It holds up your head and lets it swivel around in cool ways. Without a neck, your head would probably just fall off. And it's something you're not supposed to break. That's why this prank is so great. It *sounds* as if you're cracking your neck, but you're really just crushing an empty water bottle under your arm.

Ingredient

An empty water bottle (the kind that's made of thin plastic works best)

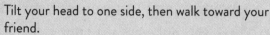

PULL THE PRANK

 Hide the empty water bottle in your armpit.

Tilt your head to one side, then walk toward your friend.

Talk to your friend as if nothing is wrong. If she asks what's going on, tell her you have a stiff neck. Make up a story, such as you've been studying and now your neck hurts because it's been in a book for so long.

 As the conversation continues, tilt your head the other way and, again, act as if nothing's wrong. When your friend asks what you're doing, tell her your neck just can't hold up your head anymore. It definitely needs cracking. Mention that your aunt is a chiropractor (a fancy doctor who straightens out crooked bodies) and that she showed you how to crack a neck. When she did it, it looked easy, so you think you'll try.

 Wrap your free hand (the one on the side that doesn't have the water bottle) around your head.

 Push your head one way and then the other. (Be gentle, your neck really is delicate!) When your head is bent, quickly smash the water bottle under your arm and make a horrified face.

 After the ghastly cracking sound, open your eyes wide as if something really bad happened. Remain still for a second, then whisper a quiet, "Now it's stuck." Look at your friend with fear in your eyes and say, "Do you think people will notice?"

Now it's time to practice adding body movements to a scene so you can make your prank more believable!

YOUR TURN!

Find a long mirror so you can see your whole body. Then act out the situations below by flailing your arms, stamping your feet, craning your neck, twisting your legs, and wiggling your middle.

You're pretending you bumped up against Bigfoot in the woods, and now you're trying to get his gross hair off your clothes.

You're pretending you're out of breath because a bear with yellow fangs chased you for three miles.

You changed your friend's ringtone to an annoyingly loud train whistle, and he never changed it back. Now people keep calling him.

You're pretending you ate a spoonful of mosquitoes, and now your stomach is flipping.

You're excited because it's April Fools' Day, the best day of the year!

You spent five hours explaining to your little sister how you did the "Crack Your Neck" prank, and she still doesn't get it. She asks you to explain it again, but you can't because you're dizzy from talking so much.

You're pretending you were cleaning the bathroom, and you got cleaning goop in your eyes.

Your friend put Bubble Wrap under the carpet, and you're jumping around trying to find a noise-free spot to stand.

 You set up a horrid stink bomb, and for some reason, your friend can't smell it, but, boy, you can!

You jump back in fear because your friend put a picture of his head in a jar and made it look frighteningly real!

 Because you've been working so hard on your pranks, you haven't slept in two days, and now you're so tired you can't stand up.

You're pretending you ate a moldy potato that gave you stiff-limb disease, and now you can't bend your arms or legs.

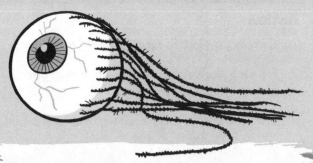

RIP YOUR EYEBALL OUT

Kids are used to a few strands of hair falling out, a fingernail ripping off, and even baby teeth wiggling out—but eyeballs? *No!* They usually stay put in those little sockets at the top of your head. We say *usually* because, with this prank, they don't. For this one, you'll attach fake eyeball guts to a plastic eyeball and make it look as if you're ripping the whole thing out of your head. This prank is unusual and fun, but definitely not for your squeamish friends!

Ingredients

- A fake plastic eyeball (you can buy a bag of these at a joke, party, or discount store)
- Ruler
- Scissors
- 20 inches of red yarn
- Clear nail polish

Action

1. Cut the yarn into five pieces, each 4 inches long.

2. Rip each piece of yarn lengthwise so each piece becomes about ten thinner strands.

3. Paint the sides of the eyeball with clear nail polish.

4. While the nail polish is still wet, stick the thin strands to the sides of the eyeball so they look like eyeball guts.

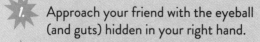

PULL THE PRANK

1. Approach your friend with the eyeball (and guts) hidden in your right hand.

2. Complain that your eye is itchy. Rub it with your hand and then with your arm.

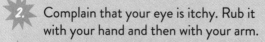

3. Bring your right hand toward your eye, with the eyeball still hidden.

4. Raise your left hand and grab hold of the eyeball guts.

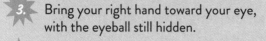

5. Announce that you can't stand your eye anymore, and start pulling the fake eyeball away from your face with your right hand, while still holding the guts with your left hand.

6. Continue to pull the eyeball out, shuddering and shaking with every yank.

 7. Pick your friend up off the floor, because he surely will have fainted by now!

Bonus Prank:
WRONG SHOULDER

A quick prank you can try any time is the classic tap-the-wrong shoulder trick. It's simple, but foolproof. All you have to do is stand behind your friend and to one side, then tap his shoulder on the other side. He'll turn toward the shoulder you tapped and find no one there. Gets them every time!

CRACK YOUR NOSE

You didn't think the geniuses at **SHMOP** would stop at cracking your neck, right? If you did, you don't know us very well. The **SHMOP** masters have figured out innovative ways you can pretend to crack your nose, fingers, back, and toes—which is fun to do and also rhymes. For this prank, you can pretend to crack pretty much any body part while biting down on an uncooked piece of macaroni.

Pre-Prank Prep

Ingredient

A piece of uncooked macaroni

Action

Practice cracking your body parts, as explained below.

1. Put the uncooked macaroni in your mouth so your friend can't see it. Be careful not to swallow it!

If you're pretending to crack your:

- Nose—Push your hand against your nose and bite down on the macaroni at the same time so the sound seems to come from your nose.

- Back—Push your hand against your back and bite down on the macaroni at the same time.

- Toe—Bang your foot against a wall or pretend to trip as you're biting on the macaroni.

- Finger—Bash your fist against a table or wall at the same time you're biting the macaroni.

 Howl and carry on as if you really broke a body part. Remember: It's your reaction that sells the prank.

Bonus Prank
BLACK EAR DISEASE

During a busy day, our hands can get dirty, or even our feet, but our ears? They usually stay clean and shiny. That's why this prank is so great: Your friend will wind up with unexplainable black gunk on her ears. When your friend's not looking, smear black shoe polish or washable black marker on the top part of her phone, where she puts her ear. Then call her. When she puts her face to the phone, instant black ear disease!

WIGGLY EAR DISEASE

Ears aren't things people think about a lot—unless they're wiggling for no reason. This prank tricks your friends into believing you have the dreaded wiggly ear disease, a condition that makes your ears move suddenly. This feared illness is sure to get you sympathy, attention, and possibly a long and interesting visit to the nurse's office.

Ingredients

- About 5 feet of yarn or string
- Ruler
- Scissors
- Two adhesive bandages

Action

1. Cut a piece of string about 12 inches long, and tie the ends together so the string is in a loop.

2. Use one adhesive bandage to stick one end of the string loop to the back of your right ear. Use the second to attach the other end of the string loop to the back of your left ear.

3. Loop a second string around the string that is now horizontal from ear to ear. Let the second string hang vertically down your back. The vertical string should be long enough so you can comfortably reach your hand back and tug on it.

4. When you pull the vertical string, your ears wiggle!

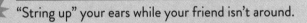

PULL THE PRANK

1. "String up" your ears while your friend isn't around.

2. Walk toward your friend without letting him see your back. Start a casual conversation.

3. Without letting him notice, slip your hand behind your back and tug on the vertical string. Tug gently at first and then increasingly harder. As you do, make your body shudder in rhythm with the tugs. Each time you pull the string, make your shoulders tic, your middle jerk, or your back stiffen.

4. When your friend asks what's happening, act worried. Tell him that you've read about wiggly ear disease and that's probably what you have. Unfortunately, it's very contagious. It leads to earlobe paralysis and hardening of the earwax. It even affects your hearing. Eventually, the only sounds you'll hear are cats fighting in garbage cans. Yikes! Your friend better back away.

107

MAGIC FINGER

You have so many fingers it can be hard to keep them all in line. And it's a pain when one of them misbehaves. For this prank, you'll complain that one of your fingers has a mind of its own, because it sticks up when you don't want it to, it refuses to text, and it twitches when you're trying to sleep. If your friend doesn't believe you, touch a bowl of soup with your misbehaving finger. All the seasoning on the top of the soup will flee to the side of the bowl because your finger is really that scary! Too bad your friend won't know that you really have dish soap on your finger and that this is a natural chemical reaction!

Ingredients

- Bowl of chicken soup (the kind that comes from a can is okay)

- 6–8 shakes of pepper, depending on the size of the holes in your shaker

- A drop of dish soap

- A plastic sandwich bag

Action

1. Put the dish soap in a plastic sandwich bag, and place the bag on your lap.

2. Put the soup in front of you. Make sure the top of the soup is flat, with only broth and no noodles or vegetables sticking up. It's okay if the noodles and vegetables are below the surface.

PULL THE PRANK

 Start with the soup in front of you. Casually add pepper, acting as if that's the way you like your soup.

 Tell your friend that everything seems to be afraid of your misbehaving finger. Crinkle your fingers and shake your hand, as if you're trying to jiggle the bad vibes out of these disobedient appendages.

 When he's not looking, dip a finger into the bag of dish soap.

 Ask your friend to watch what happens when one of your bad fingers touches something innocent, such as soup. Zip! The seasoning runs for its life!

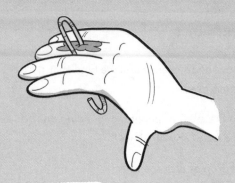

PAPER CLIP THROUGH YOUR FINGER

This is an easy, fun prank for busy pranksters on the go. All you have to do is shape a paper clip so it looks as if it's piercing your skin. Then cringe and yelp for help!

Ingredients

- Paper clip
- Ketchup packet

Action

1. Bend the paper clip into an upside-down J.

2. Dab the ketchup where the paper clip will push down into your skin.

3. Slip the clip between your fingers so the point is touching the ketchup.

PULL THE PRANK

 1. Once the paper clip is between your fingers, and you've added the ketchup blood, start acting.

 2. Let out a tiny scream, and flinch from the pain, as if someone really just hammered metal into your finger.

3. Raise your trembling hand so it's in front of your friend's face. If she offers to pull the clip out, say no. When the pain subsides, you'll be the only kid in class who can hook cool things on your hand, such as keys, earphones, and hair ties. Best accident ever!

CARTOON PHYSICS

How cool would it be to have a head that can do a 360, to jump higher when you wear your lucky pajamas, or to flatten into an accordion shape and then play accordion music with your body. Clearly, this is the ultimate in physical comedy. Cartoon characters can do these tantalizing tricks with ease, and us humans can only watch in awe. But instead of just drooling over these awesome powers, watch cartoons with a critical eye. Now that you know more about physical comedy, try to really appreciate these astounding feats of physical magic. Yes! Take that, reality!

I HAVE FOUR ARMS!

Let's face it, two arms aren't always enough. If you have only two arms, you can't feed your pet, play the violin, and text at the same time, which is unfortunate. That's why we at **SHMOP** think everyone needs four arms, which is what you'll pretend to have in this prank. When you and a friend are wearing the same shirt, and she's sitting behind you, she'll lift her arms and start combing your hair or feeding you cereal. You can just sit there, strum your fingers (your real fingers) on the table, and let your extra arms do all the work!

Pre-Prank Prep

Ingredients

Two identical long-sleeve shirts that fit you and a friend

Action

Practice in front of a mirror or with a camera timer.

1. Sit on a chair and ask your friend to crouch behind you with her head down.

2. Ask her to reach up and push your hair out of your eyes, tap your head as if you're thinking, or stroke your chin as if you're pondering something. Make faces that match her movements, as if you were really thinking or pondering.

PULL THE PRANK

 When you and your friend are wearing the same shirt, sit at a table across from the person you're pranking, such as a sibling. You can have a bowl of cereal or homework in front of you so your friend's hands have something to fiddle with.

 As you're talking to your sibling, your friend will sneak up and crouch behind you.

 Eventually, your friend will reach up and start pretending her arms are your extra arms. She'll scratch your cheek or push the hair out of your eyes as you sit there and act as if nothing is wrong. Come to think of it, she can even use her hands to finish your math homework, which would make this an even more awesome prank!

Super pranks! Now check out the next chapter to see how you can use your voice to punch up a prank!

113

FUNNY VOICES, SOUNDS, AND THE FINE ART OF GOBBLEDYGOOK

HEY, over here! It's me, behind these giant teeth.

Want to learn how to make funny sounds and speak in goofy voices? What about talk with an accent or speak gobbledygook? Well, you're at the right place, because when it comes to that stuff, I **gopher** it! Silly voices and sounds make pranks more believable; they also make them funny and more fun to pull. When I pretend my tail's caught in a tree limb, I talk in a high-pitched, squeaky squeal. When I prank that a snake is around the corner, I crinkle some leaves so it sounds as if it's slithering toward us. When I say I was chased by a scrappy hog, I sell it by making my voice as shaky as a swing set in the wind.

There are lots of ways to change your voice. You can shout, mumble, whine, whisper, or make your voice as smooth as kitten fur. You can fiddle around with tone, volume, speed, and breathiness, too. Once you nail down a few funny voices, you'll wonder how you ever lived without them! Adding sounds—such as crashing glass or banging metal—can make a prank about pretending to break a window seem more realistic.

Got it? **LOLA**-licious, give us a prank that uses a funny voice!

Let's  broke!

ANYTHING FOR SOMEONE WHO CALLS ME **LOLA**-LICIOUS. PLUS, THAT GLEAM FROM YOUR TEETH IS SO BRIGHT I DON'T NEED TO TURN ON MY NIGHTLIGHT ANYMORE. HERE YOU GO!

YOUR KID ATE MY GOLDFISH

What would your parents say if your principal called and said you were given a detention because you ate the school's goldfish? Do you think they'd ask how it tasted? Or if it went down okay? Or do you think they'd yell and

get so mad their hair would catch on fire? If you pull this prank, you'll find out. This trick involves imitating your principal or teacher and calling your parents to notify them about the unfortunate goldfish incident.

Pre-Prank Prep

Ingredient

Borrow a friend's phone. If you use your own phone, your parents will recognize the number.

Action

Practice imitating your principal. Change your voice to sound like them, but also try to copy the way they speak. Do they talk fast, slow, loud, soft, pause a lot, use specific words repeatedly, breathe heavily, or clear their throat a lot?

PULL THE PRANK

 1. Call your parents and give them the bad news: Their little sunshine ate the school goldfish. Make the story believable by using specific details, such as the time of day it happened, which classroom the goldfish was in, and a description of the teacher's astonished reaction.

 2. Tell your parent the bill to replace the goldfish is in the mail. Unfortunately, it was an exotic goldfish, and shipping a live fish from Tahiti is very expensive.

Bonus Prank:
FOOD FIGHT!

Wait for your parents to forget the call, then call again and pretend you're getting another detention for starting a food fight. Imitate a teacher this time. Apparently, you brought in something your parent cooked and everyone wanted a taste. Kids started grabbing, one thing led to another, and food started to fly. Your parent should tone down their awesome cooking abilities, because their beef stroganoff is causing havoc in the school cafeteria.

Keep reading to learn how to change your voice in a merri-marvelous way!

YOUR TURN!

Try out different voices, accents, and catchphrases to make your prank more believable, interesting, and funnier. To change your voice:

Speak with an Accent

Listen to people with accents, and try to isolate the sounds specific to the way they speak. For example, Americans and Brits treat their *r*'s differently. Americans say something is "better," whereas Brits say it's "betta." You can copy a well-known accent or make up your own by consistently pronouncing a few sounds differently.

Speak in Gobbledygook

To communicate in gobbledygook, mumble a bunch of sounds and then throw in a real word every once in a while. Make sure the word you throw in has meaning. For example, say, "Glibblie tibber blug *vampire*. Rigger robber *behind you*." Your friend will know what you mean.

Play with Sound

Experiment with different ways to change the sound of your voice:

Pitch—Make your voice:

- High-pitched, hold your head up and speak with the upper part of your throat.

- Low-pitched, lower your chin and speak with the lower part of your throat.

Breathiness—Talk with a lot of breath or no air in your stomach. Or hold your nose and talk.

Speed—Talk fast, as if your pants were on fire, or slow, as if you just woke up in a daze.

Volume—Talk in a booming voice or a whisper.

Project—Hold your head high, and make your voice shoot across the room. Then hold your chin to your chest and mumble.

Diction—Speak very precisely or mumble and slur your words.

Voice quality—Speak with a creaky, twangy, gravely, or nasal sound.

Tap into an Emotion

A big part of how your voice sounds comes from your mood. Think of how someone who's mad sounds. Or someone who's ecstatic. Try sounding like these emotions:

- Afraid
- Angry
- Bored
- Confused
- Cranky
- Disgusted

- Exuberant
- Gentle
- Hesitant
- Sad
- Serious
- Surprised

Create a Unique Style

Everyone has their own way of speaking. Some people use catchphrases, such as "gotcha" or "really?" Some people overenunciate, giggle, or mumble. Play with voices that are monotone, harsh, choppy, raspy, gravely, or droning, and figure out which works for your prank. For example, if you're pretending a waitress just put a new salt shaker on the table (even though it's really sugar), give the explanation for the salt shaker in the waitress's voice. Since the voice won't sound like you, it'll be more believable that the words were hers. And it'll be funnier!

I WANT PIZZA!

Pizza: one of our favorite topics at **SHMOP**! This prank is a triple win-win-win because it lets you practice a funny voice, trick a friend during a prank call, and talk about pizza.

 Only make prank phone calls as a silly joke. Never really pretend to be someone else on the phone.

Ingredient

Figure out what phone you'll call from. If you call from your phone, your friend will recognize the number.

Action

Practice a new voice or accent. Either make up your own or try one of these:

- <u>Nervous minion</u>—Talk in a quick, high-pitched voice. Make your voice sound nervous and shaky.

Pre-Prank Prep

- <u>Old king</u>—Talk like an important old man in a deep and gravelly voice. Add texture and growl, and say "ah" a lot in a deep voice.

- <u>Movie star with voice fry</u>—Pretend you're a too-cool movie star with a raspy, creaky voice. Try to run out of breath at the end of each sentence so your voice "fries" like bacon sizzling in a pan.

PULL THE PRANK

 Call your friend and casually order a pizza. Make it seem real by being specific about what you'd like on the pie and when you can pick it up.

 When your friend says he doesn't make pizza, tell him his number's in an ad for the town's best pizza.

 When he insists that he doesn't make pizza, ask him why he's advertising this number as a pizzeria. Keep pushing your order, and see how long you can keep it up.

YOU WON 50 BUCKS

Prank calls are so much fun we had to include a second one! This time, try to convince your friend that she'll win fifty bucks if she can say a store name in a happy, upbeat way. Unfortunately, no matter how cheerful she sounds, you'll tell her that her voice isn't happy enough. It's kind of like counting to infinity plus one— she'll never make it!

Ingredient

Borrow a phone that has a number your friend won't recognize.

Action

Practice your funny voice. Again, try to vary your pitch, breathiness, speed, volume, diction, and voice quality to create a cool, new sound.

1. Call your friend. In an excited voice, tell her she's the grand prize winner. If she says she didn't enter the contest, tell her everyone in town was automatically entered.

2. To claim the prize, she needs to say she loves the store, using the store name, in a superhappy voice. No matter how she says it, tell her it's not happy enough and she needs to kick it up a notch. See how high-pitched you can get her to go!

Bonus Prank:
IS NICK THERE?

Here's a quick and easy prank. In a disguised voice, call your friend several times and ask for Nick (or another name). He'll probably say he's not Nick and hang up. Then call back from a different phone and say you're Nick. Ask if you have any messages.

RED ANTS MAKE ME JIBBER JABBER

If you've been meaning to brush up on your jibber jabber, this prank is for you. It lets you blabber nonsense while you pretend you've been bitten by a red ant and your tongue is swelling. Start speaking in made-up words, and try to get your friend to repeat some of your nonsense. When she does, convince her she's been bitten, too!

Action

Make up words, such as *slabbebbal* and *shalabobble*, and practice saying them.

Pre-Prank Prep

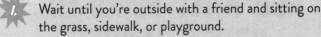

1. Wait until you're outside with a friend and sitting on the grass, sidewalk, or playground.

2. Suddenly slap your leg, as if you were just bitten by an insect.

3. Glance at your hand, and pretend you're looking at a tiny red ant. Act afraid, and say that your parent was just telling you that red ants carry a disease that makes your body swell from the inside out. Keep scratching your leg and glancing around nervously.

4. In a few minutes, gently bite down on the sides of your tongue and say, "I feel it! It's happening! My insides are swelling, even my tongue!"

5. While you're still biting your tongue, say, "It's time! We have to *slabbebbal shalabobble!*" Then, keep repeating *slabbebbal shalabobble.*

6. When your friend asks, "What's *slabbebbal shalabobble?*" look at her in panic and say (while still biting your tongue), "Now you're saying it, too! Oh no, you've been bitten!"

7. Sit back, and watch your friend get *antsy.*

BUBBLE WRAP UNDER THE TOILET SEAT

Few sounds are more awesome than the *POPPITY POP* of Bubble Wrap. These thin sheets of plastic air pockets may look innocent, but they make a big sound, especially when placed under a toilet seat.

Ingredients

- A small piece of unpopped Bubble Wrap. (You'll be tempted to pop it, but don't! Pranksters practice restraint.)
- Scissors
- Ruler
- Tape

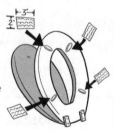

Action

1. Cut the Bubble Wrap into pieces, each 3 inches by 2 inches. Try to make each piece contain as many unpopped bubbles as possible.

2. Lift the toilet seat, and locate the "bumps" on the underside of the seat. Tape the Bubble Wrap over these bumps, then gently lower the seat.

PULL THE PRANK

After you rig the toilet seat, hang out near the bathroom and wait for the *POP, POP, POP!*

MUSICAL BUTTON MADNESS

Musical buttons are annoying little gizmos that every prankster needs in their bag of tricks. These buttons are the tiny devices inside greeting cards that play a few bars of a song when pressed. Since these gadgets are small, you can hide them almost anywhere and press them without your friend's noticing, and the music seems to come from nowhere! Priceless!

Ingredient

A musical card. The button in each card plays a different song, such as "Happy Birthday," a classic tune, or a silly jingle. Pick the one that works best for you.

Action

Remove the button from inside the card.

1. The field is wide open here. You can hide the button anywhere. Here are two ideas:

- Get a button that sings "Happy Birthday," and hide it under the carpet. Tell your friend that your pet has really good karma. When he goes outside, the sun comes out and the flowers lift their heads. It just so happens that today is your pet's birthday. You bet that somehow the universe will sing to him. Then try to get your pet to sit on the spot where the button is. If your pet doesn't cooperate, step on the spot yourself when your pet is in the room.

- Place a button on a seat, under a napkin, or under a thin pillow. Wait for your friend to sit down!

IMITATE, NEVER MOCK

Never use imitation to mock another person, or someone who is having a hard time. If you're imitating someone, keep your eye on them and make sure they're having a good time. If they're not, stop right away. Apologize, then don't do it again.

ANIMAL NOISES FROM A BOX

Everyone expects a box to just sit there. A box usually doesn't talk, walk, jump out at people, or make weird noises. But when pranksters are around, things are different. This prank takes the classic jumping-out-of-a-box trick and supersizes it to include weird animal sounds.

Ingredient

A box that's big enough for you to hide in

Action

Practice imitating the animals and insects listed below.

- barking dog
- buzzing bee
- cawing crow
- chirping bird
- clucking chicken
- cooing pigeon
- croaking frog
- gobbling turkey
- hissing rattlesnake
- honking goose
- meowing cat
- quacking duck
- screeching bat
- squawking bird
- squeaking mouse
- twittering bird

PULL THE PRANK

1. Hide in the box, and close the flap at the top as best as you can. Wait for someone in your family to come into the room.

2. When a family member enters, be patient. Don't start making noise right away.

3. When someone settles in a chair, make a quiet animal noise. Slowly increase the volume until your family starts wondering where the noise is coming from.

4. When a family member gets close to the box, thrust your arms out of the top and scream!

Bonus Prank:
WEIRD NOISES UNDER A BED

Hiding under a bed and making noise is another prank that every prankster needs to know because it's easy and fun, and scares the bejingles out of most people. It's like hiding in a box, except you'll hide under a bed, wait for a family member to enter, make some type of creepy sound, then spring out!

BOOM! I BROKE A WINDOW!

A sudden loud crash makes people jump, and we can see why. It means something broke, someone tripped, or . . . there's a prankster around. Play a loud crashing sound on your phone or computer and *pretend* you broke a window. Wait for family members to come running!

Ingredients

- A ball
- A phone or computer that can download a sound
- A crashing, cracking, smashing, or whacking sound

Action

Download the sound on the phone or computer.

 Only download sounds if your parent or guardian allows you to.

 Set up the phone or computer in the room where you'll pretend the accident is.

 Casually walk past your parent with the ball in your hand, making sure your parent notices.

 If they ask you to take the ball outside, say you will, you just want to check something in the other room.

 Go into the room with the phone or computer, and play the crashing/smashing sound loud enough for your parent to hear it.

 When they come running in, say something like: "Broken windows aren't that bad. They let lots of fresh air in, right?"

Isn't playing with your voice and sound super-di-looper? Now turn the page and learn some of the best stuff at **SHMOP**: How to trip and walk into walls!

TRIPPING, WALKING INTO WALLS, AND GOOFING OFF LIKE A BOSS

GREETINGS, recruit! It's Dr. Crankshaw, the sassy, saucy scientist who hops with the hippest. It's time to roll up your sleeves (and your pant legs, too), because things are about to get looseygoosey. I'm going to teach you how to walk into walls, slip, and trip. I mean actually stumbling over something and making it look as if you're hurt without, of course, really getting hurt.

Walking into a wall is a spiffy trick of making a noise—such as banging your foot against the wall—and then reacting all quivery, as if you're hurt. If you do it right, your friend will hear the bang and think you really walked into a wall!

Crafty, huh? It's the scientific smoke and mirrors of silly stuff.

Now it's time for **LOLA** to give us a prank. And **LOLA**, this time, be nice! We need a walking-into-a-wall prank, not a load of howdy doody.

I'M NOT GOING TO GIVE YOU A LOAD OF HOWDY DOODY. I'M SAVING ALL THE "DOODY" FOR THE NEXT CHAPTER. AND BOY, THERE ARE PILES OF IT! HEE HEE!

Piles?! That **LOLA** is really creaming my corn today. Excuse me, dear reader, my invention needs a little tweaking.

WALK INTO A WALL, SPIT OUT FAKE TEETH

Are your parents always telling you to take care of your teeth? Brush them. Floss them. You get only one set of adult teeth. Well, we're here to tell you that in the prank-o-sphere, teeth are easy to come by. Well, *fake teeth*, that is. We'll show you how to make them, spit them out, step on them, crack them, and then make a new pair. For this prank, you'll make fake teeth and also "black out" one of your teeth so it looks as if you're missing a tooth. Then you'll hide the fake tooth in your hand and walk into a wall. It'll seem as if you just lost a tooth and now have it in your hand!

Ingredients

- A tablespoon
- A tablespoon of pizza, biscuit, or crescent roll dough
- A tablespoon of flour
- A drop of red food coloring
- A drop of blue food coloring
- A drop of green food coloring
- Small mixing bowl
- Spoon
- Paintbrush or cotton swab

Action

Make a fake tooth:

1. Break off a small piece of dough.

2. Roll it lightly in flour so it doesn't stick to your fingers.

3. Shape it to look like one of your front teeth. Let it harden for at least an hour.

Make a piece that will "black out" your front tooth:

1. Break off a piece of dough, roll it in flour, and push it into the shape of your front tooth, except make it much flatter.

2. In the mixing bowl, combine the red, blue, and green food coloring to make black.

3. Use a paintbrush or cotton swab to paint one side of the flat tooth black.

4. Wait an hour* or so for the blackout tooth to dry, then press the white side of the fake tooth against one of your front teeth. When you smile from a few feet away, it'll look as if you're missing a tooth!

* If you wait longer than one hour, the white side of the tooth may not be sticky anymore. If this happens, wet the white side with water and rub it with your finger. It will become sticky again.

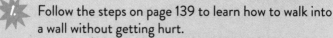

1. Follow the steps on page 139 to learn how to walk into a wall without getting hurt.

2. Press the "black out" tooth against one of your front teeth, and hold the fake tooth in your hand.

3. When your friend is near, walk toward the wall you've picked out. If your friend talks to you, answer with your lips covering your teeth, or your head turned so she can't see your face.

4. Bang into the wall as practiced. Throw your head back, scream, and put the hand that's holding the fake tooth over your mouth.

5. When your friend asks if you're okay, look down at your hand with fear in your eyes. Open your hand so your friend sees the fake tooth. Look up at her and mumble a quiet "call a dentist."

Now keep reading, to learn how the pros slip and trip and make it look natural!

YOUR TURN!

Learn how to walk into a wall, slip, trip, and bang your head!

How to Walk into a Wall

1. Pick what you'll walk into. Find a door opening you can walk past quickly or a wall that's behind a table so your friend won't see you kick the wall or stamp your foot.

2. Walk toward the wall or door opening.

3. When you're near the wall, touch your head to it, and at the same time, bang or stamp your foot.

4. Then, jerk your head back so it looks like the sound came from your head.

5. React, because that's what sells the prank. Act surprised that you hit the wall, then yell, grab your head, bend over, moan, and complain about the person who put a dumb wall in the middle of the room.

6. Practice this trick a few times before trying to fool your friend so you get the timing down and also learn how to do it without getting hurt.

How to Slip Across a Floor

1. Walk casually, then kick a heel into the floor.

2. Make that foot slide forward a little.

3. At the same time, jerk your head and shoulders back and wave your arms around like a crazy person.

4. After you regain your balance, yell, complain, and hobble around. Remember, it's your reaction that your friend will remember.

How to Trip over a Curb

1. Walk toward a curb.

2. When you're one step away from the curb, bash one foot into it so it makes a banging sound.

3. Lift that same foot quickly, and bring it over the curb. As you do, wave your arms, wiggle your body, stumble around, and—of course—complain.

How to Hit Your Head on a Desk

1. While you're sitting at a desk, put your right elbow on the desk.

2. Rest your head in your right hand.

3. Put your left hand under the desk so your friend can't see it.

4. Slowly let your right hand slide forward so your head drops.

5. When your head is about to touch the desk, bang your left hand under the desk so it sounds as if your head made the noise.

6. Gripe, groan, and grumble about how dangerous desks are nowadays.

How to Hit Your Head on a Door

1. When you hear someone knock on the door, walk toward it.

2. When you're close to the door, open it slowly.

3. Before it's open too wide, bang your foot against the door and throw your head back at the same time.

4. Hold your head, whimper, whine, and overreact like a true prankster.

 Practice these tricks, and do them carefully! If you wind up in bed with a banged-up leg, who'll be around to switch all of the cereal in your house into the wrong boxes?

HOW TO ENTER A ROOM

If your prank involves entering a room in a specific mood, always start acting before anyone can see or hear you. For example, if you're running into your house to tell the family that a mean dog is on the doorstep, don't open the door casually and then burst into hysteria, because your family will see the first calm moment and know you're pretending.

SLIP ON POOP

This prank takes effort, and when it's over, you'll be pooped—and by "pooped," we don't mean tired. We mean your right shoe will be pooped. And your left. Maybe even your hands. But don't worry; it's not real. It's poop made from some of the best stuff on earth: peanut butter and cocoa powder. To pull this prank, make fake poop and place it outside. Then walk by the poop with a friend and pretend to slip on it. Then get really gross: bend down, pick off the end of the poop, and taste it.

Action

1. Make a fresh batch of fake poop by following the peanut butter and chocolate recipe on page 156.

2. Place the poop somewhere outside where you'll be walking in the next hour.

PULL THE PRANK

1. Make an excuse as to why you and your friend need to walk to where the poop lies in wait.

2. Mention that you've been feeling dizzy. This will make it seem more realistic when you slip in the poop.

3. Once you reach the poop, step into it with one heel, slide the foot forward, wave your arms in big circles, look shocked, and yell something like *mama pajama*!

4. Once you regain your balance, tell your friend you're wondering what you just slipped on. Bend down, and examine the poop. Break off an end of the gross stuff, and pop it into your mouth. Chew on it thoughtfully, and tell your friend it's definitely fresh poop, not like the stale, dried poop you ate last week.

> Do not pull this prank on someone with a peanut allergy or even near someone with a peanut allergy. If you're not sure if your friend has an allergy, skip this prank and trick them with something else, such as the "Rip Your Eyeball Out" prank on page 101. As far as we know, no one's allergic to eyeballs.

THE RULE OF THREES

Funny things happen in threes. For example, if you step on a rake and the handle hits you in the face, it's funny. However, it's even funnier if you then hop around, twist in a circle, and step on it a second time, and then a third.

DROP A PRICELESS HEIRLOOM

Most kids have stuff in their house that shouldn't be dropped, such as little figurines from the china cabinet, fancy trinkets from the living room, and Dad's beloved bobblehead collection. For this prank, convince your friend that the trinket you're holding is a priceless heirloom, even though it's not. Then do what a true prankster would do: pretend to trip, slip, and drop the superexpensive piece in a big, showy, crash-bam-boom way.

 Don't drop something valuable, sentimental, or anything that belongs to another person. When it comes to dropping things, use your head—in addition to your feet, arms, and a big, loud "Oh no!"

Ingredients

- Find something that looks valuable and is breakable. You can find things such as little statues, picture frames, ceramic pumpkins, Santas, and bunnies at dollar stores and pharmacies.

- Create a humdinger of a story about the trinket. Make up details, such as what country it's from, how old it is, and what makes it original and valuable to your family.

Action

Practice tripping, as explained on page 140.

PULL THE PRANK

 As you talk to your friend, lead him near the curb or ledge that you've practiced tripping over.

 Tell him the story about the trinket and why your family treasures it so much.

 Once you have him convinced you're holding something priceless, walk toward the curb and trip over it.

 As you're tripping, scream and throw your hands in the air. This will, of course, send the cherished heirloom crashing to the ground and . . . uh oh . . . breaking into little pieces!

BANG YOUR HEAD, SPIT OUT BLOOD

Too much studying can make your head hurt, your mind foggy, and your eyes blurry, and if you're a prankster, it can make you spit out blood.

Ingredients

- Mixing bowl
- Spoon
- Tablespoon
- A plastic sandwich bag
- 4 tablespoons of tomato paste
- 1 tablespoon of water
- OPTIONAL: 1 teaspoon of maple syrup

Action

1. Make fake blood by mixing together the tomato paste and water. To make the blood darker and muckier, add maple syrup.

2. Use the spoon to put the mixture into a plastic sandwich bag.

3. Practice banging your head on a desk as explained on page 141.

PULL THE PRANK

 1. When you're sitting at a desk studying with friends, have the bag of fake blood handy. Then start crabbing about how all this work is making you feel foggy.

2. Go to the bathroom or someplace private, and slurp the fake blood into your mouth. Don't swallow it.

3. Sit back down at the desk, and rest your head in your hand.

4. Gradually let your hand slip, and pretend to bang your head on the desk with a loud thump.

5. Look up suddenly. Moan and hold your head as if you really just broke it.

6. Start hacking, then spit out the fake blood.

7. End by telling your friend this confirms it. You always knew studying was hazardous to your health. Now you have proof!

WHAT IS A PRATFALL?

A pratfall is when you purposefully fall to make someone laugh. It's usually an exaggerated fall, with arms and legs flailing and a great big *Ahhhh!* Literally, the word means "to fall on your butt" since "prat" is an old-fashioned term for "butt."

BASH YOUR HEAD, VOMIT GREEN GOO

Desks aren't the only things pranksters bang their heads on. Doors are fun, too. For this prank, wait until your friend is coming to your house. When he arrives, pretend to bang your head on the door and then spit out green goo you've been hiding in your mouth. He'll be glad he came to see you.

Ingredients

- Measuring cup
- Mixing bowl
- Mixing spoon
- Fork
- ½ cup of water
- A packet of unflavored gelatin
- ¼ cup of light corn syrup
- 3 drops of green (or any color) food coloring

Action

1. Ask an adult to help you boil a half cup of water.

2. Pour the boiling water into the mixing bowl, then slowly sprinkle in the gelatin packet, stirring constantly.

3. Let the gelatin sit on the counter for fifteen minutes.

4. Add the ¼ cup of light corn syrup and three drops of food coloring.

5. Stir the mixture, then refrigerate for an hour.

6. When cooled, stir the mixture with a fork so you get little chunks of colored goo.

 Even though the goo is made from all edible ingredients, don't swallow it. It's thick, and you could choke on it.

7. After you've made the goo, practice banging your head on a door as explained on page 142.

PULL THE PRANK

 Once your friend is near, put a little goo into your mouth.

 After she knocks, begin to open the door and pretend to bang your head on it.

 Then fully open the door so your friend can see your reaction.

 Act as if you're off balance, make your eyes spin in circles, let out a yelp, and then slowly let the goo leak from your mouth.

Now turn the page and learn how to add the gross-out factor to your pranks!

GROSS-OUTS:
Burps, Farts, and Big Honking Nose Blows

CLEAN the floors. Scrub the desks. Wipe the mustard off the cat. That's all I hear. Why, oh why, did I take a cleaning job at a school that pranks with vomit, bird turds, and bloody limbs? And that's the school's *good* part. Want to know about the *bad* part? It's in the **Grand Hall of Farts**. This is a place you smell before you see. It's the biggest museum of fart sounds, shapes, and smells in the world. It's a barking blowout of **brown thunder**.

Even though our cleaning crew complains about it, you can supercharge your pranks by adding a gross-out factor. Try a big wet sneeze; gurgling fart; snorting burp; warbling gulp; or loud, honking nose blow. A prank where you're pretending you just ate forty-seven hot dogs is more convincing if, in the middle, you pretend to cut a real stinker. A prank where you're pretending you have a wet, sloppy cold is pricklier if you let off a fake watery sneeze on your friend's neck.

Don't limit your pranks to gross body stuff—try pranking with other things that are sticky,

sludgy, slushy, mushy, or gushy. A good prank surprises someone with something that doesn't feel or smell as it's supposed to. Imagine putting your foot in a shoe filled with bubble soap or sniffing a fresh batch of cookies that smell like the bottom of your backpack instead of cinnamon.

See how gross-outs can be a *blast*? **LOLA**, give us a prank, and make sure it's tricky and icky!

I LOVE COOKING UP A SLIME FEST. *KABOOM!* HERE YOU GO!

A prank about sneezing out snot! Very disgusting!

IT'S SNOT FUNNY

Your friend may think this prank is *snot* funny, but we at **SHMOP** think it is. It really is. This trick involves filling your hand with hand sanitizer and then sneezing into it. When you move your hand away, you'll have "snot" on your face and in your hand. Gross! Everyone knows that's not where snot belongs. The place it belongs—obviously—is on your friend's desk.

Pre-Prank Prep

Ingredient

A handful of hand sanitizer

Action

Before you start, scope out a place where you'll wipe the "snot." Look for a hard surface that's easy to clean, such as a desk, lunch table, or locker.

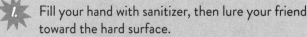

1. Fill your hand with sanitizer, then lure your friend toward the hard surface.

2. Talk to him as if nothing is wrong. When he pauses, and is looking at you, sneeze into your hand—the one that has the sanitizer.

3. Scrunch up your face in a worried expression. Slowly take your hand away from your face, and look down at your hand.

4. Yell "EEW," and say something like: "How did I sneeze out a whole bowl of snot?!"

5. Wipe your hand on the solid surface, and continue with snot puns, such as, "This is snot right" and "This is so snot funny" (even though it is).

6. In the end, confess that the goop is really hand sanitizer and that you were just trying to help him clean his desk.

Now clean your hands—which should be easy because they're already filled with sanitizer—and turn the page to learn how to make some of the grossest stuff on earth: poop!

YOUR TURN!

Pick Your Poop!

Want to know how to make fake poop? We have you covered. Really covered. Since fake poop is key to pranking, we decided one recipe wasn't enough. So here it is, a Poop-a-ganza!

Peanut Butter Poop

Ingredients

- Measuring cup
- Mixing bowl
- Mixing spoon
- ¾ cup of powdered sugar
- ⅔ cup of peanut butter
- 2½ tablespoons of cocoa powder
- Dish

Directions

1. Mix the three ingredients together in the bowl until the mixture is a big brown blob.

2. With your fingers, tear off pieces from the blob and mold them into fake poop.

3. Put the poop on a dish, and refrigerate it for an hour.

 Do not pull a prank using this poop on someone with a peanut allergy or even near someone with a peanut allergy.

Gooey Poop

Ingredients

- Measuring cup
- 1 cup of flour
- ½ cup water
- 1 cup salt
- Mixing bowl
- Mixing spoon
- 3 drops of red food coloring
- 3 drops of green food coloring
- 3 drops of yellow food coloring
- Dish

Directions

1. Combine the flour, water, and salt in a bowl, and stir.
2. Add the food coloring (all three colors).
3. Stir the mixture.
4. With your fingers, tear off pieces from the blob and mold them into fake poop.
5. Put the poop on a dish, and let it air-dry. As it dries, the outer coating will crack and make it look even more like the real thing!

Put the peanut butter poop and gooey poop outside or on a hard surface—such as a floor, counter, or desk—that can be easily cleaned. Don't put these on soft surfaces, such as carpets or blankets, because these can both stain.

Tissue Roll Poop

Ingredient

All you need for this recipe is the cardboard tube inside of a toilet tissue roll—and someone to blame.

Directions

1. Tear the cardboard roll into smaller pieces.
2. Hold the pieces in your hand, and run them under a stream of warm water. As you do, keep smooshing the pieces.
3. Once the cardboard pieces are soft, mold them into pieces of poop.

FAKE POOP ON THE TOILET SEAT

Now that you've made piles of poop, let's put some to use! For this prank, all you do is lay some of your premade poop plops on the toilet seat. That's it! Just walk away, and let the power of poop take over.

Ingredients

- Fake poop that you've made using one of the recipes on pages 156 and 157.

- OPTIONAL: A few drops of honey

Action

1. Lay the fake poop on the toilet seat or on the floor near the toilet.

2. To kick it up a notch, put little drops of honey near the poop so it looks as if the seat is covered in both number one and number two!

1. Set up the fake poop and honey, and wait for the screams!

Bonus Prank:
SNOWMAN POOP

All living things poop, and that includes snowmen. Well, come to think of it, snowmen aren't exactly living and don't actually poop, but we think they should. For this prank, slip a few round white Styrofoam balls under the next snowman your friend builds. When the sun comes out, and the snow melts, all that will be left are a few little round white snowman poops!

TOO MANY BEANS!

If you live on planet Earth, you've probably heard this song:

Beans, beans, they're good for your heart.
The more you eat, the more you fart.
The more you fart, the better you feel.
So eat beans at every meal.

That song inspired this prank, which involves making a stink bomb and hiding it in a place where your friend can smell it but can't see it. Then pretend you've eaten too many beans, and now your stomach hurts and . . . she better back away!

Ingredients

- Plastic container with a lid that seals tightly
- Tablespoon
- Mixing spoon
- A raw egg
- 2 tablespoons of milk
- 2 tablespoons of vinegar

Action

1. Crack the egg into the container.

2. Add the milk and vinegar.

3. Stir the ingredients in the container.

4. Seal the container tightly, and put it in a warm place that's out of sight, such as the back corner of your closet. Leave the "stink bomb" there for at least a few days so it can ferment. It won't smell bad right away.

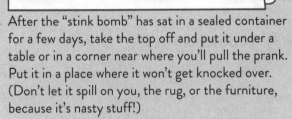

 After the "stink bomb" has sat in a sealed container for a few days, take the top off and put it under a table or in a corner near where you'll pull the prank. Put it in a place where it won't get knocked over. (Don't let it spill on you, the rug, or the furniture, because it's nasty stuff!)

 Once the smell is in the air, start groaning as if you have a stomachache. Call your friend into the room.

 When she enters, you won't have to say anything. The smell will say it all. Just keep holding your stomach and grumbling. If you feel words are necessary, mumble: "Beans! Beans! Too many beans!" She'll get it. And then she'll *get out!*

FOUR FABULOUS WAYS TO MAKE A FARTING SOUND

If you learn only one thing from **SHMOP**, it should be how to make a farting sound. If you attempt to move into adulthood without mastering this valuable skill, they send you back. Not kidding. So put your thinking cap on and get ready to light up the room!

 Mouth—(three ways)

- Make a tight circle with your mouth, then blow quickly.

- Close your lips tightly, then blow out of one side.

- Put your mouth on your arm. Make sure your lips touch your arm at all points, then blow.

2. **Hands**—Wet both palms with water, and put the palms together. Then twist quickly and squeeze out the air between your palms.

3. **Armpit**—Put a dry hand under your armpit. Make sure your hand is touching your skin with a tight seal. Slap your arm down quickly.

4. **Electronic**—If you have a cell phone or computer, download fart sounds and incorporate them into your pranks.

 Only download sounds from the internet if your parents allow you to.

THE OFFICIAL FART LEXICON

Since farts are key to pranking,
we've classified them into nine
official categories.

The Quick Rip

The Backdoor Breeze

The Long Dry Hisser

The Squeak

The Drizzy Squirt

The Silent Stink Bomb

The Loud Popper

The Whinney Whopper

The Better Crack a
Window

STICKY SYRUP SOAP

Farts, poop, and snot aren't the only gross-outs you can add to a prank. This prank combines the stickiness of pancake syrup with the ordinary activity of washing your hands.

Ingredients

- Liquid soap dispenser (which can be empty)
- Plastic container
- Pancake syrup

Action

1. If the dispenser is filled with soap, pour the soap into the plastic container and set it aside.

2. Refill the soap dispenser with pancake syrup. (Don't waste too much syrup. Only put in enough so syrup will come out when the pump on the dispenser is pushed.)

This one's simple; just set up the syrup soap bottle, and sit back and wait for someone to decide they need to get clean. Too bad their wish won't come true!

BIRD TURD BLOWOUT

Birds have no respect for people's property. They fly around thinking only about their own business, and *doing their business*. And bummer, a flock just flew over your house. They must have been coming from a giant bird smorgasbord, because *KAPOOWIE*, they lost it—all over your driveway!

Pre-Prank Prep

Ingredients

- Measuring cup
- Teaspoon
- Mixing bowl
- ½ cup of whipped cream
- 4 teaspoons of black pepper
- Turkey baster

Action

1. Combine the whipped cream and pepper in a bowl.

2. Stir slightly so the cream and pepper are partially mixed. It looks realistic when the mixture contains some gray and some white portions.

3. Squeeze the bulb of a turkey baster, and stick the tip of it into the mixture. Then release the bulb. The cream-and-pepper mixture will pull up into the baster.

4. Point the turkey baster at the surface you want to cover, and squeeze for a cool splatter effect! Study the illustrations below for examples of how these raunchy splatters should look.

Turd Splatter

Turd Plop

Turd Drip

Turd Drizzle

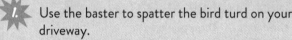

1. Use the baster to spatter the bird turd on your driveway.

2. Put on your best "holy flying birds" face, and run toward your parents.

3. Start your story with a kicker, such as: "I tried to save our property, but . . . *yikes!*" Explain that you were outside playing when you heard a strange flapping sound. It started low and got louder. Then the sky darkened, as if a storm were brewing. When you dared to look up, you saw about one hundred— no, one thousand—big black birds, squawking their heads off and flying over the house. You closed your eyes and didn't open them until the birds were gone. Then everything seemed okay—that is until you saw the driveway. Stop there. Stare at your parents with big eyes.

4. At this point, your parents will surely run outside. Follow them.

5. Act concerned and worried as you look over the driveway. If you're feeling daring, stick your finger in the "turd" and give it a taste. Tell your parents that it tastes salty and creamy and that it probably came from a crow. No wait, a blackbird. No wait, a pigeon. Yes, that's it, you're positive it was a pigeon because of its strong pigeon-y taste.

MUSHY BANANA HANDSHAKE

Serious businesspeople know the importance of a firm handshake. The right one can get you a job. Respect. A fancy office. For this prank, you'll need a great handshake—one that is firm and commanding and contains a mushy banana. An icky banana handshake won't get you an important adult job, but it should get you a laugh. Or at least a really digusted "*Eww!*"

Ingredient

½ of a banana (or any soft fruit or vegetable)

Action

Put the banana in the hand you'll shake with, then close your fist gently.

Pre-Prank Prep

PULL THE PRANK

1. Walk up to your friend, and say something like: "Hi, buddy."

2. Hold out your hand, as if you want to shake hands, but keep the palm side slightly down so he doesn't see the banana.

3. Shake your friend's hand firmly. When he pulls away, look down at your hand and say, "Oh, wow. That's where I left my banana."

SNEEZE ON A FRIEND

For this prank, you'll flick water on the back of your friend's neck as you pretend to sneeze. He'll think you showered him with wet, sloppy germs and be totally grossed out!

Pre-Prank Prep

Ingredient

Water bottle filled with water

 When you have the water bottle with you, wait until your friend turns his back.

 Cup your hand, and fill it with water.

 Make a loud sneezing sound, and at the same time, use your hand to flick the water onto the back of your friend's neck.

 When he turns around with a horrified look, tell him to calm down. You were sick only twenty-nine days last month; he has nothing to worry about.

MOUSE DROPPINGS ON THE COUNTERTOP

Mice are cute little critters, but their droppings—that's another story. A trail of teeny brown pellets in your kitchen means a bunch of these adorable little guys crawled around looking for crumbs and stayed long enough to poop the Oregon Trail across your countertop. Yuck! For this prank, make your own mouse droppings, sprinkle them on the countertop at night, and wait for someone in your family to wake up to the gross surprise!

Action

Follow one of the recipes on pages 156 and 157 to make poop. Instead of molding the brown goop into human-size poop, form it into tiny pellets.

 Make the mouse droppings when the person you'll prank isn't around.

 Once the person you're pranking has gone to bed, sprinkle the droppings in a trail across the kitchen countertop. To be extra gross, drizzle the droppings on a piece of fruit or piece of bread so it looks as if the mice had a party on the food.

 The next morning, get up early enough to enjoy the reaction!

 If you make the poop that uses peanut butter, don't pull this prank on someone who has a peanut allergy or even near someone with a peanut allergy.

PRESENT ON A PILLOW

Wouldn't it be nice to find a $100 bill or a beautifully wrapped present on your pillow? That would be great—too bad this prank doesn't do that. Instead, this prank leaves fake vomit on a pillow. But, because pranksters are such nice people, this vomit is rubbery and reusable, not the mushy, gushy kind that's hard to clean off. We at **SHMOP** worked extra hours to develop this special vomit so you can get lots of mileage out of this rubbery disk of grossness.

Pre-Prank Prep

Ingredients

- Measuring cup
- ½ cup of school glue
- A drop of red food coloring
- A drop of blue food coloring
- A drop of yellow food coloring
- A few tablespoons of nonperishable food, such as oatmeal, raisins, crackers, and crushed nuts
- Wax paper
- Cookie sheet

Action

1. Pour the glue into the measuring cup.

2. Add a tiny drop of red, blue, and yellow food coloring into the measuring cup, and mix well. The glue will turn brown.

3. Put the wax paper on a cookie sheet.

4. Pour three-fourths of the brown glue onto the wax paper.

5. Crush up the food, then sprinkle it on top of the glue. Add the food mostly in the center, then scatter some around the edges.

6. With a spoon, shape the vomit so it's not a perfect circle and looks real.

7. Pour the remaining fourth of the brown glue onto the top of the crushed food so it seals the top.

8. Wait about twenty-four hours* or until the glue is dry.

9. Peel the vomit off the paper.

* If the glue isn't dry in twenty-four hours, ask an adult to bake it in the oven at 350 degrees for five minutes. The glue will be smelly, so put the fan on and keep the kitchen ventilated.

 All you have to do is place the fake vomit somewhere that it shouldn't be (which is pretty much everywhere). Put it on a sibling's pillow, a couch, a countertop, a car seat, or a chair, then sit back and wait for the fireworks!

FULL OF BALONEY

Some people say pranksters are full of baloney. What they mean is, pranksters are full of tricks and tall tales. But what they don't realize is, pranksters sometimes are literally *full of baloney!* For this trick, you'll stuff baloney into the toe of your friend's shoe and sit back and wait for the long "Eeeeeeeeeew!"

Ingredient

A few slices of baloney (if you're fresh out of baloney, try ham and cheese, pepperoni, or another type of lunch meat)

 When your friend isn't looking, stuff the baloney into the toe of his shoe.

 Act as if nothing's wrong when he begins to slip his foot into his shoe.

 Once he realizes there's something slimy in there, act surprised. Ask: "No tomato? Mayo? Soft, yummy bread?"

 Only stuff baloney into shoes that you can clean easily. If your friend has a pair of fancy leather shoes that he wears to meet the Queen of England, don't use that pair.

Now that you're up to your eyeballs in grossness, it's time to move on! Turn the page to learn how to make annoying things you can use in pranks!

PROPS AND RIDICULOUS THINGS YOU CAN SQUIRT, HONK, AND QUACK

A BIG, beautiful birthday cake! Why don't you blow out the candle?

That was a lame attempt, try again.

Ha! You can't blow it out! And it's not because I'm a drawing in a book—well, maybe that, too—but really it's because I'm a **trick candle**. Just when you think you've gotten rid of my light, I relight! And then relight again! I'm one of those classic **prank props** that put the "annoy" in "annoying." The "trick" in "tricky." The "ick" in "icky"!

I'm here to talk about using props in your pranks. Think: whoopee cushion, bottle of hot sauce, or plastic chattering teeth. And props don't have to be stuff you buy in the store. Lots of times the things you make yourself are even better.

I know, let's ask **LOLA**. Show us how to prank with a homemade squirt ring!

SURE THING, TRICK CANDLE. JUST REMEMBER TO TAKE THE DAY OFF WHEN IT'S MY BIRTHDAY. I DON'T NEED YOUR SHENANIGANS ON TOP OF MY CAKE.

Good try, **LOLA**, but no can do. I'm saving up all my relighting energy so when it's your birthday, I can put the "irk" in "irksome"!

SMELL THE FLOWER

People love flowers because they look pretty, smell nice, and don't squirt water all over the place. But people have never been around *this* kind of flower. For this prank, you'll attach a flower to a ring. When your friend tries to smell the flower, you'll squirt her with a water balloon that's hidden in your hand!

Ingredients

- A small balloon
- A flower, either fake or real

Action

1. Fill up the balloon halfway with water. To do so, put the mouth of the balloon on a faucet and turn on the water slowly.

2. With your palm facing down, place the half-filled balloon between two fingers, and let the mouth of the balloon stick up through your fingers.

3. Put a flower between the same fingers so your friend can't see the mouth of the balloon. Partially close your fist so you're hiding the balloon but not squeezing the water out.

PULL THE PRANK

 Approach your friend with the water-filled balloon in your fist, and the flower between your fingers.

 Show your friend the new ring. Mention how great the flower smells, then sniff it yourself.

 Put your hand out, and ask if she wants to smell it. When her face is close to the flower, squeeze your fist and squirt the water at her. If she looks confused, say something like: "Wow, that flower has power!"

Gotta love those homemade props! Keep reading to learn how to make your own.

181

Picture this:

You're holding squeezable ketchup and mustard bottles when your friend walks toward you. You point the bottles at him and SQUEEZE. Out shoots what looks like wicked sprays of condiments! But your friend won't get *sauced* because what fires out of the bottles are just long red and yellow strings.

Ingredients

- Empty squeezable ketchup and mustard bottles
- About 36 inches of yellow yarn
- About 36 inches of red yarn

Action

1. Uncap both of the bottles.

2. With your fingers, thread the red yarn through the ketchup cap.

3. Tie a small knot at the top and a larger knot at the bottom of the yarn.

4. Put the excess string into the ketchup bottle, and put the cap back on the bottle.

5. Repeat steps 2–4 with the mustard bottle and yellow yarn.

6. To practice, hold both bottles away from your face and squeeze. The yarn flies out the top!

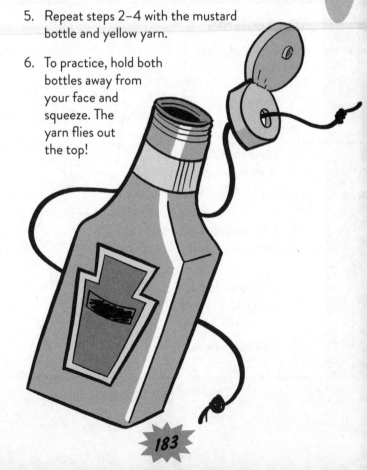

183

CRAZY DUCK QUACKS

Ducks seem innocent enough. They just swim around and do their own thing. Well, all ducks except for the crazy, out-of-control one in your neighborhood. This prank involves telling your friend that you keep seeing a wacked-out duck on your lawn, and when you and he are looking for it, startling him with a loud duck quack.

Ingredients

- Sheet of paper
- Ruler
- Scissors

Action

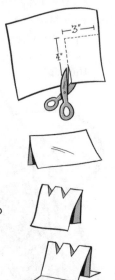

1. Measure a 4-inch by 3-inch rectangle on the paper, and cut it out.

2. Fold the paper in half lengthwise.

3. On the folded side, cut two triangular notches.

4. Fold back the sides.

5. Slip your fingers between the folded flaps, like this:

6. Hold the paper to your face, and blow into it. The result: a weird quacking sound that would irritate even your rubber duck.

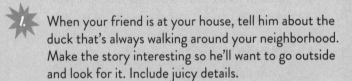

PULL THE PRANK

1. When your friend is at your house, tell him about the duck that's always walking around your neighborhood. Make the story interesting so he'll want to go outside and look for it. Include juicy details.

   - If he asks if it's an actual duck, tell him, "Yes, it's a real duck. Like a duck-duck. But no goose."

   - Stress that you both better go outside and chase the duck away to save its life.

2. When you're outside, let your friend get a little ahead of you.

3. Take out your paper quacker, and honk away!

SODA GUSHER

Every prankster needs a soda gusher in his toolbox. It's pretty much a staple in the prankiverse. However, the gusher you'll build in this trick is no ordinary one. You'll pretend that your water bottle is one of those inanimate objects in futuristic stories, and gushes with a mind of its own!

Ingredients

- Bottle of iced tea or lemonade that isn't see-through
- Five scotch mints
- 3 inches of clear tape
- Soda

Action

1. Drink the iced tea or lemonade. Refill the bottle two-thirds of the way with soda.

2. Attach the scotch mints to one end of the tape, and leave the other end free.

3. Lower the strip of scotch mints into the bottle, but don't let the candy touch the soda right away.

4. With a quick hand, drop the scotch mints into the drink and recap the bottle.

 When you're outside with your friend, pull out the drink.

 Tell her about the crazy sci-fi stories you've heard about how one day inanimate objects will come to life and start bossing us around. Add juicy details, such as how our cars will drive us where *they* want to go and our refrigerators will keep food only *they* like and kick out the rest.

 Hold up the drink bottle, and tell her that in the future, even harmless drinks like this will come to life. If the drink doesn't want to stay in the bottle, it'll gush out on its own.

 Hand her the bottle so she can see for herself. When she opens the bottle, and the drink gushes out, act surprised. Then keep going on about how sci-fi stuff is coming true!

 Pull this prank outside; it's a messy one!

CHEESE CURL CRAZINESS

Cheese curls are a modern scientific marvel. They're crunchy, delicious, and always fun to prank with. Did you know you can slice one open, fill it with something disgusting, and mold it back together with water? The geniuses at **SHMOP** have been dissecting cheese curls for years, trying to figure out what gives them this astounding remolding ability. We haven't identified any specific ingredient, so we've concluded that it's magic, pure and simple. Try this prank if you're ready to test cheese curls' magical abilities by cutting one open, filling it with something gross, and feeding it to an unsuspecting friend.

Pre-Prank Prep

Ingredients

- A few fat cheese curls (the fatter the curl, the easier it is to work with)

- A table knife

- A toothpick

- Something to fill the curl with, such as salt or sugar—or if you're feeling spicy, cayenne pepper

Action

1. Slice a curl lengthwise.

2. Use a toothpick to gently carve out the center of one half of the curl.

3. Sprinkle salt or sugar into the cavity you just created.

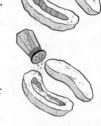

4. Dip your finger in water, and use your finger to wet the cut side of the half that wasn't filled.

5. Push the two sides back together, matching them up as best as you can so the curl doesn't look as if it was cut.

6. Hold the pieces together firmly until they stick.

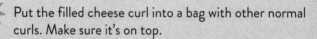

PULL THE PRANK

1. Put the filled cheese curl into a bag with other normal curls. Make sure it's on top.

2. When you're talking with a friend, reach into the bag and munch on the normal curls. Lick your lips, and comment on how delicious they are.

3. When your friend asks for one, hold out the bag. If he doesn't pick out the filled one right away, let him take another until he gets it.

4. When he spits it out, act flabbergasted. These curls are a delectable treat! Perhaps his taste buds are backfiring and he's no longer capable of appreciating fine food?

Pre-Prank Prep

THE WORLD'S LONGEST CHEESE CURL

Since the geniuses at **SHMOP** have been studying cheese curls for so long, it would be a shame to use these little scientific wonders in only one prank. So here's another. In this trick, you'll use cheese curls' astounding reattaching ability to build a few of the world's longest cheese curls. Then brag to your friend about how your family has invented an incredible new technology that quickly grows things such as plants, vegetables, even cheese curls. When your friend questions this, whip out proof—a few monstrously long cheese curls!

Pre-Prank Prep

Ingredients

- About two dozen fat cheese curls
- A table knife

Action

1. With the knife, slice the rounded ends off a few curls.

2. Put water on your finger, and use the water like glue to connect two sliced curls. Hold the pieces together for a few seconds so they stick together.

3. Keep going until you have a few preposterously long curls. Make sure the long curls all have rounded ends so they look believable.

NOTE: If you're going to take the long curls anywhere, such as school, transport them in a plastic container or clean box, because they're delicate.

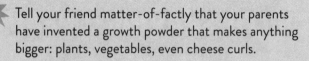

PULL THE PRANK

1. Tell your friend matter-of-factly that your parents have invented a growth powder that makes anything bigger: plants, vegetables, even cheese curls.

2. When she questions you, assure her that it's true. In fact, the powder could be worth billions. All your parents do is sprinkle the growth powder on something, water it with a tiny spray hose, and cover it carefully. In a few days, the thing has quadrupled in size.

3. When your friend questions you again, take out your colossally long curls. Tell her these curls were regular size just yesterday.

4. If your friend is *eating up* the story, tell her she can have a cheese curl, but if she does, she'll grow, too. She should start with just a nibble because she could grow so big she won't fit into her house and will have to sleep in the backyard for the rest of her life.

Bonus Prank:
SNACK BAG FILLED WITH SHAVING CREAM

Here's a quick and easy prank that also involves salty snacks. Start with two snack-size bags of chips or pretzels. Eat the food from one bag, then fill the empty bag with shaving cream. When you're sitting at lunch, put both bags on your lap so your friend can't see either. Start eating from the one that's full of real snacks. When your friend asks for a taste, hold out the bag filled with shaving cream. He'll have a soggy surprise!

SPILLED MILK

Did you ever hear the saying *don't cry over spilled milk*? With this prank, you won't cry over it, you'll laugh over it. Use white glue to create a reusable milk spill that you can place on your friend's keyboard, backpack, phone, or anything else that should not get wet. When your friend sees the mess, she may actually cry over it!

Ingredients

- White glue
- Sheet of wax paper
- Ruler
- Blunt knife

Action

1. Place the wax paper on a table.

2. Slowly squirt the glue onto the paper so it looks like the milk spill on page 193. Make sure it's at least ¼ inch thick; if it's too thin, it will be see-through.

3. After at least ten hours, and when you're sure the glue is dry, use the knife to lift up the edges of the glue splatter. Once all the edges are lifted, peel the splatter off the wax paper.

 Place the rubbery spill on your friend's keyboard, backpack, phone, or anything else that's hard to clean.

 When your friend notices it and gets upset, tell her she's literally crying over spilled milk and, let's face it, she's too old for that.

Pre-Prank Prep

FAKE MOUSE ACROSS THE FLOOR

For this prank, you'll drag a fake mouse quickly across the floor when someone in your family is nearby. You're sure to get a loud "EEK!" and it won't come from the mouse!

Ingredients

- Fake mouse, which you can buy at a joke, party, or discount store

- A few feet of invisible string, which you can buy at a fabric or discount store

Action

Tie the invisible string around the mouse's nose so you can pull it forward.

PULL THE PRANK

1. Put the mouse on the floor, under a couch or table or behind a doorway.

2. Call the person you're pranking into the room. Talk to him as if nothing were wrong.

3. When the time is right, yank the string so it looks as if a real mouse were zipping across the floor!

Bonus Prank: MOUSE DROP

Fake mice are little critters with lots of scare, so don't put the prop away yet! Try placing it in a cabinet so when someone in your family opens the door, the mouse drops in front of their face. Tie the loose end of the invisible string around a sturdy cup, and make sure the other end is still attached to the mouse. Put the cup in the cabinet, and place the mouse on the very edge of the shelf. Close the cabinet door. When someone in your family opens the door, they'll get more than the cup they're looking for!

Bonus Prank:
MOUSE ON MY LEG

A fake mouse is too cool to use only twice. Recycle it by making it look as if it's crawling up your leg! When you're wearing loose pants, such as pajama bottoms, put the mouse on the floor and bring the invisible string up through your pants. Hold the string in your hand, and call your friend into the room. When your friend notices the mouse, scream and throw your hands in the air. When you do, the invisible string will pull, and it'll look as if a real mouse were crawling up your leg!

STUFF THAT'S NOT TRUE, BUT WE WISH IT WERE

HEY, it's me, Jill Chill, just hanging out, watching the boats go by. I never worry about anything. The only thing that sometimes knocks me off my game is when a coconut falls on my head, which happens . . . let me think . . . oh yeah, every day.

One thing I never do is make a big deal about getting facts right, because pranksters don't take facts seriously. Just the opposite, they rely on misinformation. Fabrication. Exaggeration. Showstopper whoppers.

Pranksters use false facts, made-up lists, and pretend articles to trick their friends. Try it yourself! You can make a fake menu for your favorite restaurant featuring dishes such as tree-bark pancakes and cream of toenail soup. You can read a pretend article to your parents about a new travel agency that will take you on a tour of the local sewer plant. Or read an announcement about a new parent-teacher bonding initiative that will send your teacher to your house to help with the dishes. And if you're having trouble finding really cool, totally made-up junk, look no further. **LOLA**'s got handy lists of nonsense you can use to prank your friends. **LOLA**, lay some of this stuff on us!

ANYTHING FOR YOU—MY GAL PAL WHO ALWAYS KEEPS IT REAL, THE PERSON WHO INVENTED CHILL!

A list of tips on how to lower family expenses? That's great, **LOLA**, something we can all use!

HOW TO LOWER
FAMILY EXPENSES

Adults always talk about how expensive things are. Don't waste money, they say. Don't leave the lights on. Don't buy 500 PlayStation games when we don't even have a PlayStation. To quiet this chatter, we've created a list of money-saving tips you can photocopy and read to your parents. (Or take a picture of the tips and read from your phone.) Start by agreeing with your parents that the family needs to cut back. A night or two later, announce that you—being the responsible, mature kid that you are—have come up with a list of ways to lower expenses. Read the list in a serious voice, and see how far you can get before your family realizes you're pranking them.

Five Ways to Lower Family Expenses

1. **Get a cow.** Instead of using an expensive lawn mower, buy a cow that can walk around and chomp off the grass for free. If you don't have a lawn, keep the cow inside for free milk, valuable manure, and bragging rights to the coolest pet on the block.

2. **Reuse Q-tips.** Why use a Q-tip once and then throw it away? Use it at least a dozen times to save about 0.0000023 cents per day.

3. **Sell the minivan.** No one can agree on who should sit where, and the car most likely smells like old milk anyway, so you might as well ditch it and save a few bucks. Instead, walk, ride your bike, or attend things virtually. When you attend virtually, you don't have to wear shoes and socks—another money saver.

4. **Sell the good china.** Let's face it, only Mom likes the good china. Everyone else is afraid to touch it. Do the family a favor by selling it and buying big plastic bowls that no one can break.

5. **Join a warehouse store.** Buying in bulk saves money. If you're wondering if you really need 5,000 pounds of potato salad, a twelve-person sauna, and a 72-pound wheel of cheese, the answer is yes, of course you do.

Make up your own handy lists of hogwash, and try to convince your friends and family that they're true. When you do, follow these guidelines.

Five Fantastic Tips for Making Up Stuff

1. Start off realistically. Begin your story with facts that sound real. Hook your audience with a sincere attitude.

2. Gradually exaggerate facts. Don't jump into the nonsense too quickly. Slowly build the ridiculousness so your listener wonders if you're fibbing but doesn't quite know.

3. Follow the "of course not" rule.
If your listener questions whether the story is made up, say "of course not" at least once and keep the prank going.

4. Use facial expressions and body language.
Facial expressions, body movement, gestures, voice inflection, and props will make your story pop and keep your audience listening.

5. End with a bang.
Once your friend realizes they're being pranked, use it as an opportunity to make them laugh (or groan). Throw in a few lines of pure silliness that couldn't possibly be true but are really funny anyway.

STUDENT OF THE MILLENNIUM

Wouldn't it be great if you got your school's Student of the Day award? What if you got the Student of the Week, Month, or Year award? But wait—what if your school had a Student of the *Millennium* award, and you got it?! You'd have bragging rights for an entire 1,000 years! It's fun to imagine that, and your parents' reaction if their little prodigy was selected for this incredible honor. Photocopy the letter on the next page, or retype it and print it, and read it to your parents. As you do, hold your head high and puff out your chest, because you're the most awesome student since the Middle Ages!

Student Of the Millennium

Dear Parent or Guardian,

The faculty and staff are pleased to inform you that your child has been chosen as our Student of the Millennium. This prestigious award is granted to a student who exemplifies academic excellence; superior citizenship; and a positive, can-do attitude. Your child was chosen after a rigorous search since this award is bestowed on a student who is the most exemplary in the past 1,000 years.

We selected your child despite reservations from the gym teacher, who frankly was not impressed during the square dancing segment of our curriculum. The teacher noted that your child dances like a daddy longlegs creeping across a driveway full of slugs—but you know, in a good way.

Despite the dancing, we are impressed with your child overall, especially their ability to fit fifty-four chocolate candies in their mouth while whistling "The Star-Spangled Banner." So we decided we'd roll with it!

Congratulations again on this prestigious achievement, and we wish you and your child much success in the future.

Sincerely,

M. Curie
Principal

HELP WANTED: PLEASE DO MY CHORES

Pranksters are busy people. They spend a lot of time practicing pranks and pulling them. They don't have time for chores. To solve this problem, post an ad for someone who can work for you. Read over our sample text below, then create your own help-wanted ad. Try to convince your parents that you're serious and that they need to advertise this job. After all, someone's got to do the dishes.

Hardworking Kid Needed!

Wanted! Happy, cheerful kid who likes to work hard even though he'll never get paid. Must be able to load and unload the dishwasher, walk the dog (or cat, fish, hamster), fold the laundry, clean mud off my shoes, and clear gross stuff out from under my bed. Must be good at removing ketchup from everything (including sibling's hair). Looking for someone who will do each chore thoroughly; there's no middleman here. If you have time, please do my homework, too. Must be able to spelll and rite correctly.

WOW, I'M A MILLIONAIRE!

Cereal boxes often contain more than just cereal. They can include toy surprises, treats, and prizes worth millions of dollars. Okay, maybe million-dollar prizes are rare in your neighborhood, but they're common in the prank-o-sphere. This trick involves printing a certificate that looks like a winning sweepstakes ticket and slipping it into your family's cereal box. As your sibling sleepily munches on his morning meal, sit back and wait for peals of joy. Then, help him celebrate his big win!

Action

Photocopy the ticket on the next page, and slip it into the cereal box.

THE WE LOVE CEREAL
Sweepstakes!
WINNING TICKET!
Congratulations!

You are the grand prize winner of the We Love Cereal Sweepstakes! You have won a year's supply of cereal, which is equivalent to fifty-two boxes. You also won a tour of our innovative facility in Grand Rapids, Michigan. Last, but certainly not least, you won **ONE MILLION DOLLARS!**

To claim your prize, please go to www.cerealsweepstakes.yum. Click the I AM A WINNER button, and fill in your information. We will contact you about how you can claim your prizes!

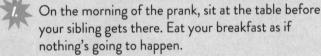

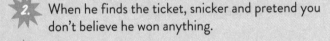

1. On the morning of the prank, sit at the table before your sibling gets there. Eat your breakfast as if nothing's going to happen.

2. When he finds the ticket, snicker and pretend you don't believe he won anything.

3. After a minute or two, look at the ticket yourself and pretend you're starting to believe he really won. Tell him you've heard of this contest; they talk about it on TV all the time. Wonder out loud if winning this prize means no school for a week? Or no homework? Surely millionaires don't do homework!

Bonus Prank:
FROZEN CEREAL

Stop! Do you still have the cereal out? If so, try our "Frozen Cereal" prank. At night, pour your sibling's favorite cereal into a bowl and add milk. To make it look real, put a spoon in, too. Then put the bowl in the freezer. The next morning, when your still-sleepy sibling stumbles to the breakfast table, put the frozen cereal in front of him and announce that you made breakfast. If he asks why, say it's because you wanted to do something "special" for him.

OPERATION NO MORE SPINACH

Do your parents make you eat healthy food? Do they talk endlessly about vitamins and minerals, spinach, kale, and blah, blah, blah, yadda, yadda, yadda? Well, we have new information, written by really important smart people, saying that kids no longer need to eat vegetables. Photocopy the news article on the next page or take a picture of it with your phone and read it to your parents. Tell them that the article lists the government's new nutritional guidelines. Who knows, maybe this will get you out of eating something you don't like tonight!

USDA Makes New MyPlate Nutritional Recommendations

Foods We're Aspiring Toward

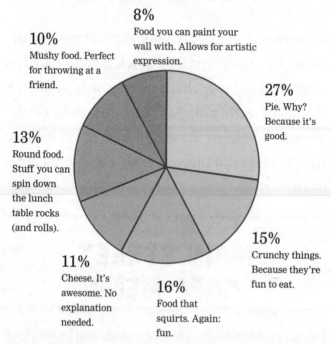

8%
Food you can paint your wall with. Allows for artistic expression.

10%
Mushy food. Perfect for throwing at a friend.

27%
Pie. Why? Because it's good.

13%
Round food. Stuff you can spin down the lunch table rocks (and rolls).

11%
Cheese. It's awesome. No explanation needed.

16%
Food that squirts. Again: fun.

15%
Crunchy things. Because they're fun to eat.

The United States Department of Agriculture (USDA) recently updated nutritional guidelines for children in the wake of compelling new research. New studies show that children should eat more fruit, protein, and healthy fats. Foods that are no longer recommended are:

- Green vegetables, such as spinach, kale, and lettuce, which make kids fart and get caught in their teeth.

- Hard foods, such as raw beets and potatoes. According to the USDA, if it can dent a car, you shouldn't eat it.

- Mystery foods, such as stews and casseroles. The USDA claims that if we don't know what's in it, we shouldn't eat it. Use your head, America!

211

CANDY THAT'S NOT CANDY

If you're trying to get your friends and family to eat healthier, try this quick prank. Unwrap a dozen pieces of hard candy, and refill the wrappers with grapes. Twist the ends of the wrappers back in place. Then offer the treat to your friends and literally trick them into eating healthier!

MAIN STREET CAFÉ MENU

Do the restaurants in your neighborhood have boring menus? Are their "specials" no longer special? The staff at **SHMOP** understands. That's why we've been working with top chefs at fancy restaurants to come up with innovative offerings. Either photocopy the menu here or take a picture of it with your phone, then read it to your parents the next time they're debating where to stop for dinner. This will surely make their stomachs turn!

Main Street Café Menu

A restaurant that redefines what technically can be classified as food.

Appetizers

Shoe Leather Sliders

Assorted Crackers with Earwax Dip

Baby Wipe Flatbread

Fried Parsley and Grass Nuggets

Tater Tot Turd Bites

Entrees

Peanut Butter and Nose Hair Sandwich

Uncooked Pasta with Raw Mushrooms

Canned Cheeseburger (still in the can)

Toothpaste and Cheddar Melt

Beef and Broken Pencil Stew

Giant Jar of Baby Food (extra blah flavor)

Frozen Broccoli on a Stick

Steak (cooked in the 1990s, but we think it's still good)

Desserts

Rat Pudding with Truffle Sauce

Hardened Gelatin (hard enough to bounce)

Sticky Sardines in Cinnamon Sauce

Red Cabbage Brownies

Lemon Cake with Lip Balm Icing

Drinks

Beef and Berry Slurpee

Shaving Cream Shake

Root Beer Mayonnaise Float

Tuna Fish Tea

Toenail Soda

Water (extra charge if you want it clean)

Yum! Your mouth is probably watering after reading that menu. Wipe the drool from your chin, and turn the page to learn why it's important to practice your pranks!

PRACTICE, PRANK, REPEAT

HOWDY doo! You made it! You've pranked your way through our entire school. Doesn't time fly? At **SHMOP**, it flies like a shoe slipping in poop, but it does fly. And humdinger, look at you! Your head is still attached, your neck isn't cracked, and you have only a teeny dot of fake vomit on your chin. Well done!

There's only one more thing you need to know if you want to be a top-notch prankster: practice, practice, practice. (Okay, that's three things, but you get it.) Practice a prank until it seems believable, the same way a magician rehearses a magic trick. If you want your parents to believe you've been chosen as the Student of the Millennium, rehearse your story in front of a mirror. Then practice explaining the story to a buddy who's in on the trick. When you rehearse, you become confident—and as cool as a pillowcase—and that's rooty-tooty in the prank-o-sphere.

Okay, hold on to your hat, I'm going to go all corn pop on you now. **LOLA**, give us the quiz that'll determine if this recruit is plucky enough to be a Prank Master Supreme!

FINE, HERE'S YOUR QUIZ. BUT THEN SLOW YOUR ROLL. HOW MANY TIMES DO I HAVE TO TELL YOU, A *LAUGH OUT LOUD APPARATUS* NEEDS HER BEAUTY REST?

Boy, today you're really razzing my berries. New recruit, excuse me for a minute. Turn the page, and take the quiz while I straighten out my invention. And when I say "straighten," I mean *straight* to the canning factory!

THE FLIMFLAM EXAM

If you pass the exam below, you will have the right to call yourself a **Prank Master Supreme** and have automatic bragging rights for a full year.

Question: What is the main ingredient in fake vomit?

A. Meat loaf

B. Green juice

C. Carrots

D. Your sister's soggy cereal, which has been in the sink since last Tuesday

Answer: This is a trick question. The answer is anything that's gross and mushy.

Q: Is it possible to eat too many beans?

A: Is it possible to have too much good luck? Use your head.

Q: What happens to kids who never learn how to make a fart sound?

A: The rules about learning to make fart sounds are clear: The kid cannot graduate into adulthood. If you haven't mastered this skill yet, turn back to page 162 and get crackin'.

Q: I want to try the "Mushy Banana Handshake" prank, but I don't have a mushy banana. What should I do?

A: Pranksters don't give up easily. You should find something else, such as the potato that's been in the back of the fridge for three weeks, put it in your hand, and get the job done.

Q: If you pull Smashing an Orange Slice Through Your Head and your friend really believes you did this, you should:

A. See if he wants to buy the Brooklyn Bridge

B. Tell him the Eiffel Tower is currently 50 percent off

C. Take his temperature, because his brain is probably melting

D. Stick close to this poor kid, he needs a good friend to look after him

A: D. Even though pranksters like silly tricks, they're good kids who look after their friends.

Q: Match up the official fart classification
with the correct illustration:

The Drizzly Squirt

The Whinny Whopper

The Quick Rip

The Loud Popper

A: From top to bottom: The Quick Rip, The Whinny Whopper, The Loud Popper, The Drizzly Squirt

Q: Can the "Never-Ending Pee" prank really
go on forever?

A. Yes   **B.** No

A: Yes. The scientists at *SHMOP* have been testing this prank since 1979, and based on our time-modeling algorithm, we predict that it can truly continue until the end of time.

218

Q: Which prank prop is the most annoying?

   A. Soda Gusher   **B**. Ketchup and Mustard
                            Squirt Machines

   C. Fake Mouse   **D**. Spilled Milk
     Across the Floor

A: This is another trick question. They're all superannoying, and therefore, all awesome.

Q: What if I think this exam stinks? There's no way these questions can tell if I'm a Prank Master Supreme.

A: This is an exam in a prank book. Did you think this would be real? If you did, go back to page 1 and reread this entire book.

If you got a bunch of these right, you are an official **Prank Master Supreme**! Congratulations, fellow prankster!

Back so soon? **LOLA** and I were just, um, *discussing* how to end this tour.

HHUURR GRRRGGH.

YES, WE'RE *DISCUSSING* IT.

Um, ignore those terrifying groans, **LOLA**'s just hungry.

GRRR RUUUHH RRRAAAGHHH HHUMMPH

Holy ravioli! She sounds like an ad for stomach medicine. Sorry, dear girl, there's nothing I can do but a total **RESET!** Take cover, **LOLA**'s going to explode. That is, explode with **PRANKS**!

MAGIC PEN

Imagine Dr. Crankshaw and other **SHMOP** geniuses visiting your school to talk about their scientific research on vomit, cream doughnuts, and fake snakes in the toilet. What if, at the end of the talk, Dr. Crankshaw handed out magic pens for everyone to take home? Well, try to picture that happening, because that's the story you'll need to pull this prank. Tell your parent that a crazy scientist visited your school and gave you a magic pen. When your parent asks if the pen is really magical, demonstrate its mysterious ability—it can bend water!

Pre-Prank Prep

Ingredients
- Plastic pen
- Fluffy towel

Action

1. Rub the sides of the pen vigorously back and forth across the towel. When you do this, the pen picks up an electrical charge from the towel.

2. Turn on a faucet so the water drizzles in a thin stream. If too much water comes out, the trick won't work.

3. Hold the pen near the stream, but not so close that the pen gets wet. The stream of water bends toward the pen because of its electrical charge.

PULL THE PRANK

 With the pen and towel in hand, approach your parent or guardian, such as your mom, with a worried look. Tell her a strange scientist spoke at your school and gave everyone a weird pen to take home.

 As you talk, rub the pen against the towel. If Mom asks what you're doing, say you think there are germs on the pen and you're trying to rub them off.

 Tell her the pens are special because they're made from old TVs and leftover cell phone guts. They're weird, but they're supposed to have really good karma.

 When Mom questions the pen's special properties, tell her it's so powerful it can bend water. Turn on the water, and let a thin stream flow.

 Move the pen toward the water, and say, "See? Good karma." Then let out your best mad scientist laugh.

223

SOMEONE PEE-D!

No one likes pee on the floor, because it's smelly, germy, and gross. But one kind of pee isn't so bad. The scientists at **SHMOP** are proud to have formulated an *upgraded* pee that doesn't smell, isn't gross, and is okay to prank with. To make our pee, draw the letter *p* a dozen times on paper, cut out the *p*'s, and spread them across a room. Then yell to your family that's there's *p* all over the floor!

Ingredients

- 12 sheets of paper
- Scissors
- Pencil

Action

1. Draw a dozen or more *p*'s on paper.

2. With scissors, cut out the *p*'s.

1. Scatter the *p*'s on the floor in one room when your family's in another part of the house.

2. Run into the room where your family is, and start yelling about pee on the floor. Tell everyone they better come look.

3. Follow your family into the room, and wait for the laughter!

Bonus Prank:
BROWNIE BUST

Try the same trick except with brown *e*'s. Cut out a dozen *e*'s on brown paper. Put the *e*'s on a fancy dish, cover them with tinfoil, and offer the brown *e*'s to a hungry friend. If you tell him you made them yourself from directions you found in a book, you won't be lying!

UNDRINKABLE DRINK

What's better than a cool drink after you've been running around outside? Not many things, as long as you can actually *drink* the cool drink. Too bad your friend won't be able to sip this one, because it's a cup of gelatin that only looks like a drink. When your friend tries to sip from the straw, she'll get a whole lot of nothing!

Ingredients

- Mixing bowl
- Whisk
- Measuring cup
- 3-ounce box of gelatin
- Clear glass
- Straw

Action

1. Ask an adult to help you boil 1 cup of water.

2. Whisk together the hot water with one 3-ounce packet of gelatin in a mixing bowl.

3. Add 1 cup of cold water to the mixture, and whisk it in.

4. Pour the mixture into the glass.

5. Place the straw in the gelatin so it looks like a drink.

6. Put the glass of gelatin in the refrigerator for two to three hours.

PULL THE PRANK

1. This one's easy—put on your most innocent face and hand the gelatin drink to your friend.

2. When she can't slurp up the drink, act surprised. Drinking through a straw is easy, didn't she learn how to do that when she was a toddler?

Bonus Prank:
UNSPILLABLE DRINK

We know pranksters are busy people, so here's a real time-saver. Reuse the cup of gelatin to trick your parents! Lay the cup sideways on the carpet, and leave it there for your parents to see. Even though the gelatin isn't spilling out of the glass, it will look as if it will, and this'll surely be startling.

Don't leave the glass on the carpet too long, because once the gelatin reaches room temperature, it will get soggy and leak onto the carpet. Then the trick will be on you, because you'll have to scrub out the stain!

DOLLAR BILL MIND BENDER

It's fun to win money and sad to lose it. The good thing is, with this bet, you'll always win because your friend won't be able to figure out the trick. Place a dollar bill on a table and an upside-down bottle on top of it. Then bet your friend he can't get the bill out without touching the bottle or knocking it over. If he tries all the normal ways, he won't be able to do it. But you will because you'll know the secret, which is slowly rolling up the bill and using it to gently push the bottle forward. Ha! Take that, gravity!

228

Ingredients

- A dollar bill (or any denomination)
- Unopened plastic water bottle or empty glass bottle. (If the bottle is too light it will fall over.)

Action

1. Place the bill on a flat surface and the bottle upside down on top of the bill.

2. Start from one end and slowly roll the bill into a tight curl.

3. Once the rolled bill reaches the bottle, keep going slowly. As you continue to roll, the bill will push the bottle, and it will slide forward without tipping over.

Pre-Prank Prep

PULL THE PRANK

 Set up the bill and bottle on a table.

Tell your friend that you have hidden powers and that you can get the bill out from under the bottle without touching the bottle or knocking it over.

 Ask him to try it first. Most likely, he'll knock the bottle over.

 Then it's your turn. Use your best showmanship, and say something like: "Abracadabra, obey me, bottle." Then slowly roll up the bill.

 Once the bill is free, hold it up and say, "Ta-da. Money obeys me!"

WHAT'S S'MATTER?

Did you ever hear this joke:

> YOU HAVE S'MATTER ALL OVER YOUR FACE.

> WHAT'S S'MATTER?

> NOTHING'S S'MATTER WITH ME, WHAT'S S'MATTER WITH YOU?

That joke inspired this prank. First, tell your friend the joke. Why? Because it's funny. Then convince her that she has something on her face. She'll try to rub it off, but you'll tell her that it's still there. Then, being the good friend that you are, you'll offer her a tissue to clean it off with. However, you've filled the tissue with flour so when she uses it to clean her face, the joke will have come true, she'll have s'matter all over.

Ingredients

- Packet of tissues
- Spoonful of flour

Action

1. Open the tissue packet, and slide out the top tissue.

2. Unfold the tissue, and sprinkle flour on it. Spread out the flour so it's not all clumped in one spot.

3. Refold the tissue, and slide it back into the packet.

 When you have the tissue packet with you, tell your friend the joke.

 After she laughs, tell her, "No really, you have something on your face." She'll probably try to rub it off.

 Tell her it's still there. Hold out the tissue packet, and ask if she'd like to use one. Then, boom! *S'matter!*

ACKNOWLEDGMENTS

Thank you, Shauna Cagan, Brian Gonsar, Naomi Gruer, Marilyn Ostermiller, and Kathleen Wilford, who are my critique partners, my sounding board, my friends. Thank you for always reviewing my work patiently, carefully, and seriously—even when I ask you to read an entire chapter of gross-out pranks. Thanks especially for commenting on the fart jokes; you're right, they stink. Thank you also to improv genius Zach Mouriz of Spitfire Theatre and amazing theater actor Jeff Wittekiend for your wise advice and helpful tips on physical comedy. You guys rock!

INDEX

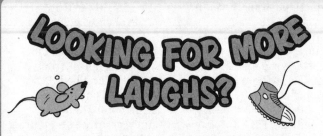

LOOKING FOR MORE LAUGHS?

Follow a cast of fictional funny experts into the Laugh Lab, a hilarious joke-building factory that teaches you how to create your own jokes, puns, silly one-liners, and more!

Each chapter explores a different style of joke making, such as surprise, contrast, and exaggeration, and includes hundreds of hilarious examples.

By the end of the book, you'll have a set of tools in your joke belt to make friends and family actually LOL.

INCLUDES MORE THAN 500 FAMILY-FRIENDLY JOKES— PLUS ZILLIONS THAT YOU CAN CREATE ON YOUR OWN!